MW01180630

THE
I ONLY NEED ONE COOKBOOK
COOKBOOK

CONTENTS:

APPETIZERS

SALADS

SAUCES

SOUPS

GRILLING

THE MAIN EVENT

CONTENTS:

I'VE GOT SOME QUESTIONS:

What do you mean I only need one cookbook?
You collect a cupboard full of beautiful cookbooks, thousands of recipes, and end up using only two or three out of every book. Why do you do that? The answer is that life is busy, and you don't have time for a lot of experimenting. And while pretty pictures of exotic entrées are fun to look at, many recipes are either too complicated, or require ingredients so unusual that you just don't bother.

What good is a recipe if you don't use it? When you serve a meal for family, friends, neighbors, clients, or your boss— you want to prepare something that you know is a sure winner. You rely on familiar favorites. Every recipe in this book will become one of those favorites— guaranteed.

What makes a great recipe?
Two things: the end product tastes great, and the recipe is fairly easy to produce with ingredients that are neither exotic nor difficult to find. Every recipe here is a guaranteed winner that you will prepare over and over again.

I don't know anything about cooking. What about me?
No worries. Even if you've never cooked a meal in your life, you can work with these easy to follow recipes. This book is for anybody who wants tips, tricks, and easy recipes that produce 5-star results.

How did you acquire this collection of can't-miss recipes?

You probably could have done this yourself—but didn't. How many times have you gone to a picnic, potluck, tailgate, birthday party, wedding, Bar Mitzvah, or other social gathering where guests brought a dish to share? At some point you sampled a family favorite and uttered those famous words, "You have to give me the recipe."

But did you follow up? Did you find a notepad and pencil, call back the next day, or send an inquiring e-mail? Probably not. But I did. While you were going back for seconds, I was nagging the host to write it down. I have tried very hard to give credit where credit is due... but there are some recipes that I have tinkered with for so long that I just don't remember where they came from.

What kind of cooking credentials do you have?

I am not a professional chef. I work in television as an anchor and reporter at the NBC affiliate in Detroit. So, I don't do a lot of cooking on the job. I occasionally make omelets for my co-workers when I work the morning show, but that's about it. However, I love to cook. For me it's relaxing, even therapeutic to put on music, pour a glass of wine to slice, dice, and sauté the afternoon away. I have gathered these recipes over many years, tweaked them to find just the right mix, and now offer them to you. You will, no doubt, make your own refinements to suit your style and tastes. That's what cooking is all about. Enjoy!

COOKING TIPS AND TRICKS

Asparagus

For tender asparagus, don't slice off the stalk ends. Gently bend a spear until it breaks. The natural breaking point will separate the tender spear from the tough end.

Avocados

It's sometimes hard to find avocados in the store that are ready to use. This is the rare fruit that you don't want to use fresh. When you get home with fresh avocados, put them in a brown paper bag, crimp the end closed, and put the bag in a cabinet for a couple of days. The avocados will ripen to perfect softness for guacamole or salads.

Bacon

Maybe you've seen this cooking tip online: *Rinse bacon under cold water before frying to reduce shrinkage by almost half.* Baloney! And, by the way, don't rinse your baloney either. Nothing makes cooking exciting (and dangerous) like mixing grease and water on a hot pan. Don't do it! I find a good way to cook bacon is on a baking pan (with a raised edge) in the oven. Bake at 350 for about fifteen minutes (longer if you like crispy). Save yourself the pain and mess of grease splatter from a fry pan on the cooktop.

Beer Mugs

This isn't exactly cooking, but it is a great idea. Invest in a set of heavy glass beer mugs and keep them in the freezer. Whether you're serving steaks off the grill or pizza, you'll put a smile on a beer-loving guest when you offer suds in a frozen mug.

Brown Sugar

To soften a block of brown sugar, seal it in an airtight container with a few apple slices, or a slice of white bread. This should soften it up within a day or two.

Need it soft right now? Put the open container of brown sugar in the microwave next to a cup of water. Heat on high power for 30 seconds.

Cooking Oils

Let me say out front that I'm not a doctor, nutritionist, or scientist. But I have done a good deal of reading about oil since I love to cook and would like to stay healthy. There is plenty of information out there about MUFA's (moo-fahs), PUFA's (poo-fahs), free radicals, and other health considerations. Do some reading before making choices. That said, I keep two oils in my pantry.

Virgin olive oil is a clear winner for me. Your grocery store probably carries twenty varieties of olive oil, but many are not what they pretend to be. The best olive oil is extra virgin olive oil because it's the purest, and offers many health benefits related to your heart and cholesterol. But to get all of the benefits, you have to find an olive oil that is *cold pressed*. The downside is that it's more expensive and you may not find it in the average grocery store. But, for salads or dipping, the flavor of a high quality, cold pressed, extra virgin olive oil is worth the extra cost.

At the bottom of the olive oil ladder are those labeled *Light or Extra Light*. By the way, the name has nothing to do with calories. All olive oils have the same calorie count. It has to do with processing. These oils are widely viewed as the lowest quality olive oil because they are mixed with refined oils. That's why *Extra Light* is often the cheapest olive oil on the shelf.

*Tip If you are going to sauté or fry, extra virgin olive oil is not a good choice. Prolonged heat breaks down the oil and ruins the consistency and taste. Here's where you need to understand *smoke point*. That's when cooking oil begins to burn. This is indicated by unpleasant smoke and my wife coming into the kitchen to open all of the windows. When cooking oil burns, it loses flavor and breaks down into nasty things that you don't want to feed yourself or anyone else.

Extra Virgin olive oil has a low smoke point (about 350°). When you fry or saute (high temperature cooking) you have several better options. I think Canola oil is best with a smoke point of about 400° and the lowest saturated fat content of any of the commonly used cooking oils. Corn oil is also a good choice. And one more thing...heat your pan first, then add oil to the hot pan. Prolonged heating breaks down the oil. Unless you're using a non-stick surface pan, then add enough oil to coat the surface before heating.

Corn On The Cob

The most common mistake with corn on the cob is overcooking. The two most common methods of preparation are boiling and grilling.

Boiling Corn: Heat a large pot of water to boiling. Peel off covering and put corncobs in the water. When water returns to a boil, cook for only 3-5 minutes. Never add salt to the boiling water. Salt makes corn tough. Try adding two teaspoons of sugar to the water when the corn goes in.

Grilling Corn: Some people grill corn in the husk. I don't for two reasons. One, it's hard to husk hot corn. And two, you miss out on the slight charring on the kernels which is pleasing to the eye. I recommend you get rid of the husk and strings before cooking. Soak the cobs in water sweetened with sugar. Cook them on a hot grill for about nine minutes (*see Sideshow section*).

Dental Floss

Keep some in the bathroom for your teeth (especially when you eat corn on the cob), and some in the kitchen for slicing. Did you ever cut into a soft cake with a fat cake knife? After the first slice the cake is smushed like a half-filled beach ball. I hate that. Use dental floss for a clean, almost invisible cut.

Eggs

For lighter, fluffy scrambled eggs, add a little milk while beating the eggs. They'll also stretch a little farther if you're serving a crowd.

Hardboiled Eggs:

To hard-boil eggs without cracking the shell: Put warm water in a pan with the eggs. Add a pinch of salt to the water and bring to a light boil. Reduce heat and cook eggs for ten more minutes. Plunge the cooked eggs in cold water immediately after cooking. Remove shell when eggs have cooled.

Fresh or Old Eggs?

Place an egg in cold salted water. If it sinks, it's fresh. If it floats, it's old. Fresh eggs have a rough and chalky shell. Old eggs are smooth and shiny.

Raw or hard boiled?

Spin it. A hard-boiled egg will spin like a top. A raw egg will wobble.

Lettuce

Use Romaine lettuce and other darker leafy greens in salads rather than iceberg lettuce. While iceberg does have some nutritional value, it has less vitamin A, C, iron, potassium, and calcium than darker greens. When you do use iceberg lettuce (sandwiches and burgers) here's a quick way to remove the core. Grasp the head by the top; firmly slam the core on a countertop. The core will cleanly pull away.

Omelets

For years I made omelets wrong. I would cook the eggs until almost done, then add the extras and flip over one half of the cooked eggs. One day, I watched a real chef cook an omelet. Start with a small lightly oiled pan. Sauté your veggies and/or meat. Add about ½ a cup of beaten raw eggs for an average size omelet. At the very end, add cheese before folding the omelet. The grilled veggies become part of the omelet, much more appetizing than raw veggies folded inside.

Onions

If you have a food processor, use it to dice onions. But if you have to chop the old fashioned way… try this to cut down on tears. Peel off the outer skin, and hold the onion under cold tap water for a minute before slicing.

Oranges

To peel an orange easily, first roll it firmly on a table top, or between your palms with firm pressure.

Perfect Pasta

I learned this trick from a chef at a fine Italian restaurant in Detroit. The worst thing about cooked pasta is that it gets sticky and globs together. **Here's the trick:** When the pasta is done cooking, pour it into a colander and submerge in cold water. If that's not possible, run cold water over the pasta removing all of the heat. If you simply set warm pasta aside after cooking, it will continue to cook and get mushy and sticky. Keep the cooked pasta in a bowl of water until it's time to serve. Just before serving, submerge pasta in boiling water for fifteen seconds, and it's ready to go, hot and fresh.

Tip: When cooking pasta, put a splash of oil in the boiling water to help keep the pot from foaming over the edge. And **never** cover a pot cooking pasta.

Quick Freeze

When you want chicken in bite sized pieces before cooking (fajitas or stir fry) try a quick freeze. Rinse boneless chicken breasts and set them out on a plate. Put the plate in the freezer for twenty minutes to make slicing easier. Use this same *quick-freeze* when making crab cakes and Christmas cookies (see recipes).

Raw Meat

Never place cooked meat on the same plate you used to carry raw meat. Bring a clean plate or platter for carrying cooked food.

Refrigerator Fresh

Put a box of baking soda in the back of the refrigerator to keep it fresh. Throw the old box down the sink to freshen the drain. Never throw away orange or lemon peel. Put them down the disposal to freshen the drain.

Rice

Avoid sticky white rice by rinsing it before cooking to remove some of the starch. For firmer rice, use slightly less water than indicted by instructions.

Sriracha

Sriracha is a type of hot sauce made from chili peppers, vinegar, garlic, sugar and salt. It's ethnic origin is unclear, though Thai or Vietnamese is the best bet. You can find it in the ethnic food section of most groceries. I use it on eggs, pasta, burgers, vegetables, salad dressings and spreads. Keep a bottle in your fridge.

Tomatoes

Peel tomatoes easily by placing them in boiling water for about a minute and then plunging them into cold water. The skin will peel right off.

Turkey Stuffing

I don't think you should stuff a turkey or chicken. While there is some disagreement on this, most cooking experts agree that your bird will cook more slowly and possibly not completely when stuffed. It's also not healthy to have your stuffing soak up raw poultry juice. Bake stuffing in a casserole. (*See the Sideshow section*).

PARDON MY FRENCH

This is the only place in the book where we'll get a little fancy... and by fancy, I mean learning some French words. Don't let that scare you. This is simple cooking. But simple ideas sound more sophisticated if you say them in French.

Mise en place (pronounced meez-on-plas). In English, the phrase means to put things in place. This simple idea is practiced in every efficient professional kitchen and you should do the same. Before you start cooking, take the time to measure, wash, chop, slice or dice everything you'll need. Set the ingredients out in the order you'll need them. There is nothing worse than getting halfway through a recipe before discovering that you're missing a key ingredient.

If you can handle a little more French, let's talk about what you can do with a roux (pronounced: roo). A roux is the foundation of so many recipes that you should learn it before we start cooking. Many of the exotic sounding sauces you find in upscale restaurants begin there. A roux is a thickening agent for soups, sauces, stew, gravy, and at least one fabulous appetizer (Spinach & Artichoke Dip).

You can make a roux with any fat or oil, but I suggest using real butter. In addition to thickening whatever it is you're making, a roux will add a light toasted flavor and a little bit of color.

> ***Tip:** Never add flour directly to a dish in order to thicken it. You'll get lumps and a starchy taste. It's the cooking of flour (in a roux) that prevents lumps and removes the starchy flavor.

THE PERFECT ROUX

Ingredients:

Whether you make one cup or one gallon, the proportions of ingredients don't change:

1 part butter

Equal part flour

Directions:

Heat butter in a small sauté pan. Sprinkle in flour and continue cooking for about ten minutes, blending and folding until the mixture turns a light golden color.

What Can You Do With a Roux?

Béchamel Sauce:
Béchamel (BEH-sha-mel) is a versatile and delicate white sauce named for Louis de Béchamel, the Marquis de Nointel… in case you were wondering. An unidentified chef who worked in Louis's kitchen invented it, but Louis got the credit. Isn't that how it always goes? Béchamel sauce can be used in many recipes including macaroni and cheese, and vegetable lasagna. It's also nice over steamed vegetables, chicken, or fish.

Ingredients:
1 cup milk
1 tablespoon butter
1 tablespoons all-purpose flour

Directions:
In a saucepan, bring milk to a simmer over medium heat, stirring occasionally and taking care not to let it boil. The milk should be warm in order to thicken. In a separate saucepan, heat butter until it melts and becomes frothy. Blend flour into melted butter a little bit at a time. Keep folding until you get a smooth golden paste. You've made a roux. Slowly add the hot milk to the roux, whisking vigorously to make sure it's free of lumps. Now you've made a Béchamel sauce. The thickness of the sauce depends on how much milk you add. That's up to you. You'll find many uses for this velvety white sauce.

Newburg Sauce:
Béchamel sauce plus garlic, tomato paste, and Sherry.

Cheddar Cream Sauce:
Béchamel sauce blended with shredded cheddar cheese (great over vegetables).

Mexican White Sauce (for enchiladas or nachos)
Béchamel sauce plus diced chilies, paprika, and shredded Monterey Jack cheese.

Velouté Sauce (Vel-oo-tay)
Béchamel sauce made with chicken, fish, or vegetable stock instead of milk. Use this to thicken soups, stews or creole. You'll be surprised how many different ways you can use these simple sauces.

THE SPICE BLEND

INGREDIENTS:

1 tablespoon ground black pepper

1 teaspoon basil

1 teaspoon garlic powder

1 teaspoon onion powder

¼ teaspoon oregano

1 teaspoon paprika

1 teaspoon parsley
1 teaspoon red pepper (cayenne)
¼ cup salt
½ teaspoon rosemary
¼ teaspoon tarragon
¼ teaspoon thyme

I put this recipe here because it really doesn't fit anyplace else, and like a roux, it comes up fairly often. You'll find a lot of specialty seasonings at the grocery store intended for seafood cooking, Cajun cooking, blackening, and grilling. Most of them are very similar and expensive. Save yourself money and make your own. The Spice Blend is a very nice all-purpose seasoning that you'll use often.

Directions:
Mix all ingredients together and store in an airtight container.

❧ APPETIZERS ❧

BRUSCHETTA AND PIZZETTA

INGREDIENTS:

6 Roma Tomatoes

2 teaspoons garlic powder

½ teaspoon salt

¼ cup extra virgin olive oil

¼ cup fresh chopped basil

1 loaf of Italian Bread

Butter

Let's get one thing straight. The French didn't invent everything that has to do with food. In France, Bruschetta generally consists of roasted bread slices rubbed with garlic and topped with extra-virgin olive oil, salt and pepper.

In Italy, Bruschetta consists of roasted bread slices topped with a mixture of diced tomatoes, garlic, olive oil and fresh basil. Now, that's Bruschetta!

While there is some debate over the correct pronunciation, in Italian, _ch_ is pronounced as a "k" sound. So, the Italian version is pronounced _brew-SKET-a_.

Pizzetta is a variation on the same theme, sort of like baby pizzas on Italian bread slices instead of baked pizza dough. Try using sausage, sun-dried tomatoes, or other vegetables like grilled red peppers, or asparagus tips. Experiment a little. Add a slice of Mozzarella cheese to melt on top.

Directions:

Prepare tomatoes first. Remove stem ends and place tomatoes in boiling water for one or two minutes. Now you can easily remove the skins. Dice tomatoes. **Don't** use a food processor for this. Put diced tomatoes in a bowl and add garlic powder, olive oil, and basil. Mix and set aside.

Preheat oven to 425°. Slice bread on a diagonal (about ½ inch thick slices). Butter lightly on both sides. Lay out slices on a cookie sheet and bake for about 5 minutes, until top starts to slightly brown. Turn them over and bake another 5 minutes.

Remove from oven and spoon some of the tomato mixture onto each slice. Sprinkle each slice with chopped basil. Serve.

** For a nice twist, top each slice with mozzarella cheese and pop back into the oven for a couple of minutes to melt the cheese.

For pizzetta: prepare bread the same way, but instead of topping with tomatoes, experiment with various meat or vegetable mixtures. Sauté some chopped mushrooms, red peppers, or asparagus. . Or, try a topping of prosciutto or thin slices of cooked Italian sausage. Finish off with a slice of Mozzarella cheese. Put the breads back in the oven for 2 or 3 minutes to melt cheese before serving.

GRAVLAX

INGREDIENTS:

A piece of raw salmon that fills the length of a casserole dish.
(Use a ceramic dish, not a tin baking pan.)

½ cup sugar

½ cup salt

1 large bunch of dill. The flavor comes from the dill, so it's impossible to use too much.

I learned how to make this Scandinavian treat while on an Alaskan cruise. The name literally means *Grave-Salmon*. Hundreds of years ago, Nordic fisherman cured raw salmon by burying it in the sand. We'll cure ours in the refrigerator. Gravlax most closely resembles lox and is served as an appetizer or maybe with a bagel and cream cheese for breakfast. By doing this yourself, the cost is about a third of what you pay for those fancy little 4-ounce packages at the grocery store.

Directions:

In a small bowl, mix together salt and sugar. Chop dill very fine. Rinse your piece of fish and place it in the casserole dish. Cover it with about half of the salt and sugar mixture. Top with about half of the chopped dill. Flip the piece of fish and cover with remaining salt, sugar, and dill. Cover the fish with plastic wrap, and place two heavy books on top to press the fillet. Put the casserole in your refrigerator for 24 hours. Remove the fillet from the casserole and rinse thoroughly. Slice very thin. Gravlax freezes well if you vacuum seal small bags. You can thaw and use a little at a time.

DO YOU KNOW YOUR SALMON?

Smoked salmon is typically hot-smoked, and has a flaky texture like grilled salmon. Lox is cured and often cold smoked. Gravlax, like lox, is cold cured, but not smoked.

**The curing process kills bacteria.

GUACAMOLE FRESCA

INGREDIENTS:

3 large avocados

1 large Roma tomato (diced)

¼ cup onions (finely diced)

¼ cup minced fresh cilantro

1 teaspoon minced jalapeno pepper

½ teaspoon garlic powder

½ teaspoon cumin

2 tablespoons lime juice

2 tablespoons water

salt and pepper to taste (optional)

The first time I tried to make guacamole, I goofed. I figured fresh ingredients meant fresh green avocados. Wrong! Have you ever tried to peel a fresh green avocado and remove the pit? Short of using dynamite, it's impossible. So, I did a little research and discovered I needed ripe avocados (ripe meaning soft, not green and hard). How was I supposed to know that? The problem is, you sometimes can't find ripe avocados at the grocery store where fresh is king. So, here's what you do.

Plan ahead. Buy fresh green avocados (those with rough, pebbly skin) and store them in a brown paper bag for two or three days in a cupboard in the kitchen. When you open the bag, like magic, they're ripe and soft— perfect for guacamole. This guacamole is light and natural because you don't add any sour cream or cream cheese. Guacamole should *never* have a dairy case, French onion, pass the potato chips sort of creamy texture. Nothing here but avocadoes, fresh veggies, and spices.

Directions:

Slice the avocados north to south, not along the equator. That makes it easier to scoop out the fruit and remove the pit. Mash with a fork to a smooth consistency.

Add all other ingredients and blend well. Cover and refrigerate for at least one hour so flavors can get to know each other. Guacamole should be on the mild side. But, if you like yours with more zip, add some spicier chiles. Serve with tortilla chips. Magnifico!

NACHO AVERAGE NACHOS

INGREDIENTS:

3 tablespoons Canola
or corn oil

1 lb. ground meat
(beef or turkey)

1 medium onion (diced)

1 tablespoon chili powder

1 tablespoon green chiles

1 large can of refried beans
1 (16-ounce) jar of your
favorite salsa *(or fresh
Pico de Pooko— See recipe)*

1 (8-ounce) bag shredded
cheddar cheese

1 (16-ounce) carton
of sour cream

1 (4-ounce) can of
green chiles or
jalapeños (diced)

I love nachos. But, for me, the worst thing about traditional nachos is that the chips get soggy, even rubbery buried under the cheese and goo. I like my chips crunchy. So, this recipe eventually morphed into something more closely related to my Italian heritage since you layer it in a casserole...like lasagna without the noodles.

This is a great dip to take with you to a potluck because it's easy to warm up once you get there, and it's neatly contained in a casserole. The only other thing you need is a bag of chips.

Directions:

Preheat oven to 375°. Heat oil in a saucepan and brown onions and ground meat together. Sprinkle in chili powder and green chiles during final minute of cooking. Pour meat mixture into a bowl and blend with refried beans. *Tip: Using 1-tablespoon of green chiles will make your dip mild. If you like it hotter, kick it up with jalapenos. Now you're ready to build your layers in a baking dish (ceramic is better than tin).

Layer one-	Meat and refried beans mixture
Layer two-	Sour cream
Layer three-	Shredded cheese
Layer four-	Salsa or Pico de Pooko

Repeat the same sequence. Bake at 375° for approximately 20 minutes. Serve hot with tortilla chips. This easily becomes a veggie dip by simply removing the ground meat from the recipe.

PICO DE POOKO

INGREDIENTS:

3 cups diced Roma tomatoes

¾ cup black beans
(drained and rinsed)

¾ cup golden or white corn
(drained)

¾ cup fresh cilantro (chopped)

½ cup finely diced onion

¼ cup diced green pepper

½ teaspoon garlic powder

½ teaspoon chili powder

½ teaspoon salt

2 tablespoons lime juice

1 tablespoon minced green chiles
(use more, or hotter peppers to
suit your taste for heat)

In recent years, salsa has risen in status from an ethnic cousin of ketchup to a highly esteemed condiment. I think it happened in the mid-1990's when North America discovered Ricky Martin and fell in love with all things Latin. Salsa and Pico de Gallo have the same basic ingredients (tomatoes and onions). The biggest difference is that salsa is more liquefied. Pico de Pooko (a name my daughters invented) brings together the best of both worlds: a spicy tomato base, but also chunky and more substantial than salsa with lots of goodies. Pico de Pooko goes great with chips, or as an accompaniment to grilled chicken or maybe Tilapia. Try spooning some over an omelet.

Directions:

Unlike salsa where a food processor is a great help, for Pico you really need to chop, dice, and mince by hand to avoid ending up with a paste. Put all ingredients in a large mixing bowl. Blend well and refrigerate for 30 minutes before serving to allow the flavors to mingle. Want some extra heat? Add a little Sriracha sauce.

SPINACH ARTICHOKE DIP

INGREDIENTS:

¼ cup olive oil

2 tablespoons (butter)

¾ cup diced onion

2 teaspoons minced garlic

½ cup flour

1½ cups chicken
stock or broth

1½ cups heavy cream

¾ cup Parmesan cheese

2 Tablespoons chicken
bouillon granules

1 Tablespoon lemon juice

1 teaspoon sugar

¾ cup sour cream

12 ounces cooked
chopped spinach

Small jar/can of artichoke
pieces (chopped)

1 cup shredded cheddar
or Jack cheese

This is my favorite recipe for spinach artichoke dip, and I've tried many of them. This dip is served warm. I developed this version because it is both delicious and relatively easy to make. And, here's the part where you feel like a real chef. For the base, first you'll make a roux, and then a velouté (vhe-loo-tay). You're a regular Julia Child!

Directions:

In a saucepan, warm olive oil and butter together. When butter has melted, add onions and cook for 3 or 4 minutes until soft. Stir in the garlic and cook for another minute. Sprinkle in flour and continue cooking for about five minutes, blending and folding until mixture is free of any lumps and turns a light golden color. Slowly pour in chicken stock until smoothly blended. Turn heat to low setting and add heavy cream, bouillon granules, lemon juice, and sugar. Blend well. Add sour cream, spinach, artichokes, Parmesan cheese and shredded cheddar cheese. Blend until smooth and serve with chips.

TOASTED RAVIOLI

INGREDIENTS:

1 bag of frozen or
refrigerated ravioli

2 eggs

1 cup of milk

Italian seasoned breadcrumbs

1 large jar of your favorite
spaghetti sauce

Parmesan cheese

2 cups of Canola oil

This is one of my favorites because it has a family connection. While details vary, no one disputes that it all started in St. Louis.

In the early 1940's, Oldani's was a popular Italian restaurant in an area of St. Louis known as The Hill. As the story goes, a chef mistakenly dropped an order of ravioli into hot oil instead of hot water. Quickly realizing his mistake, he removed the ravioli. Not wanting to waste good food he gave the plate of toasted pasta to a willing subject sitting at the bar, Mickey Garagiola (my uncle), older brother of former ballplayer and broadcaster Joe Garagiola (my dad). Mickey said, "Hey, with a little parmesan cheese and sauce, these would be great!" A tradition was born. If you ever visit *The Hill* in St. Louis, ask anybody. They'll know the story of toasted ravioli.

Directions:

Bring a large pot of water to a boil. Add ravioli and return to boil. Cook an additional two minutes. Drain and set aside in cold water. In a small bowl, combine eggs and milk. Mix well. In a separate bowl put a generous amount of seasoned breadcrumbs. Place ravioli (a few at a time) in the milk mixture, then into the bread crumbs to coat lightly. Heat oil in a medium saucepan. Add ravioli (a few at a time) to the oil. Cook about one minute on each side. You want a nice golden brown. Heat up your spaghetti sauce. Arrange toasted ravioli on a plate with a bowl of sauce in the middle. Sprinkle the ravioli with Parmesan cheese and serve.

*Tip: I like to fry the ravioli ahead of time and freeze them. That way, I don't have all the mess when company arrives. Spread them out on a cookie sheet and heat in a 400 degree oven for about ten minutes. Sprinkle with Parmesan cheese and serve.

UNDER THE JICAMA TREE

1 whole avocado (diced)

½ cup sweet corn

½ of a large red
Bell pepper (diced)

¼ cup black beans
(from a can, drained)

½ cup jicama (diced)

½ cup onion (diced)

½ teaspoons salt

1 tablespoon
minced jalapeno

Generous handful of
cilantro (chopped)

1 tablespoon lime juice

I know... there's no such thing as a Jicama tree. I just wanted to see if you were paying attention. Tell you the truth, I didn't even know what jicama was until I saw it on a menu that described this wonderful appetizer. Jicama is a crispy and sweet tuber that looks a lot like a turnip or a potato. Its origin is South American. It is very popular in Mexican food. Most grocery store produce departments will carry jicama.

By the way... when choosing jicama at the store, go for a medium size. A very large jicama will not be as sweet. This is a wonderful appetizer on a hot summer day because it's so light and fresh.

Directions:

Before dicing the jicama into bite sized cubes, peel the coarse brown outer layer as you would a potato. Mix all ingredients in a large bowl. Add the avocado last and mix gently. Now get a small bowl (about the size you might use for serving dip). Line it with plastic wrap and pack it to the rim with the jicama mixture. Cover and chill in the refrigerator for several hours or overnight. When it's time for your guests, invert the bowl on a serving plate to remove the chilled mixture. Surround this little temple of tastiness with chips and serve.

❋ SALADS ❋

CAESAR SALAD

1 head of Romaine lettuce

1 can of anchovy fillets

1 teaspoon garlic powder

1 tablespoon lemon juice

1 tablespoon Dijon mustard

1 tablespoon Worcestershire sauce

1 coddled egg (See below)

¾ cup extra virgin olive oil

¼ cup Parmesan cheese

Croutons (see homemade croutons below)

Coddled Egg

HOMEMADE CROUTONS

Preheat oven to 300°. Slice a loaf of Italian bread. Lightly butter each side of each slice. Sprinkle both sides of each slice lightly with garlic powder. Now cut the slices into generous cubes. Arrange them on a cookie sheet and bake 10 to 12 minutes. Turn them over and bake another ten minutes.

While you find Caesar salad on almost every restaurant menu, you rarely find the real thing unless you make it yourself. And once you've had real Caesar dressing, you'll be disappointed by the many cheap imitations. Let's get one thing straight right now. Real Caesar dressing *never* looks like Ranch dressing. *Creamy Caesar* is a fraud.

Many food historians credit Caesar Cardini with inventing Caesar salad back in 1924. On a busy night at his restaurant he ran short of supplies and concocted the salad with available ingredients. With a hint of showmanship, he prepared the salad at the table, still the way traditional Caesar salad is served at fine restaurants.

According to Cardini's family, anchovies were not part of the original recipe. Rather, it was Worcestershire sauce that gave the hint of anchovy flavor. So if you align yourself with the fairly large number of *anchov-a-phobes* out there, you can skip the anchovies and still call your salad authentic. But you're missing the best part.

A coddled egg will give the dressing a creamier texture than a raw egg, and it's also safer. Salmonella concerns are removed by the quick bath in boiling. To coddle an egg, bring a pot of water to a boil. Gently place the (room temperature) egg in the water and cook for 30 to 45 seconds. Rinse egg under very cold water.

Directions:

In a mixing bowl, dice anchovy fillets into nearly a paste. Blend in garlic powder, lemon juice, mustard, and Worcestershire sauce. Stir vigorously. Add a coddled egg and beat. Slowly pour in oil stirring constantly. Add Parmesan cheese and stir vigorously. Wash and trim Romaine leaves into bite-sized pieces. Toss with dressing and sprinkle on Parmesan cheese.

CURRY CHICKEN SALAD

INGREDIENTS:

4 cups cooked chicken (diced)

¾ cup mayonnaise

1 cup of (white or golden) raisins

¼ cup diced celery

3 tablespoons curry powder

¼ cup honey (use more if you like it sweeter)

I've always liked chicken salad, and stumbled upon this delicious variation at a restaurant in Scottsdale, Arizona. I didn't ask for the recipe, but studied my lunch closely to determine the ingredients. Here's what I came up with. This recipe puts an inviting spin on an old standard. Your guests will be delighted at this international twist.

Directions:

In a large bowl mix together chicken, mayonnaise, raisins, celery, curry powder, and honey. Blend together. Add a little water if it seems dry. Chill and serve.

MACA-TUNA GOOSH-GOSH

6 cups cooked
elbow macaroni
(or pasta of your choice)

1 12-ounce can of tuna
drained. (Use tuna packed
in water NOT oil)

1 cup frozen green peas
(thawed and cooked)

½ cup diced celery

2 teaspoons sweet relish

Goosh-Gosh dressing
(see recipe)

GOOSH-GOSH DRESSING

1¼ cup mayonnaise

½ cup sugar

¼ cup apple cider vinegar

¼ teaspoon celery salt

¼ teaspoon black pepper

1 teaspoon Dijon mustard

I don't know where this recipe came from. The name came from my daughters. I guess it's a cousin of tuna casserole. But this salad should be served cold.

Directions:
Cook pasta and peas according to directions on their packages. Now mix all ingredients with dressing in a large bowl. Chill and serve.

*Tip: You may not use all of the dressing unless you like your Goosh-Gosh very gooshy. Mix leftover dressing with some shredded cabbage for coleslaw.

Goosh-Gosh Dressing

Directions:
Mix all ingredients in a bowl and blend well.

MAPLE AND CILANTRO CHICKPEA SALAD

INGREDIENTS:

3 tablespoons rice vinegar

3 tablespoons lime juice

½ cup extra-virgin olive oil

¼ cup maple syrup

4 teaspoons curry powder

4 teaspoons cumin

½ teaspoon sea salt

1 medium red bell pepper diced

¾ cup golden raisins

½ cup finely chopped onion

Handful of cilantro chopped. (For my money it's hard to use too much cilantro)

2 (15-ounce) cans chickpeas rinsed and drained

Those little beige beans are best known as a base for hummus, a Middle Eastern staple. But, they answer to a variety of names (chickpeas, garbanzo beans, ceci (CHECH-ee) beans to Italians. From strictly the perspective of good health, two cups of garbanzo beans provide your entire recommended daily requirement of fiber. But even in smaller amounts they help reduce bad cholesterol. Overall, garbanzos provide powerful support for your digestive system. But enough with the Mayo Clinic tutorial... this salad borrows from several cultures and will leave your audience puzzled as to the ingredients, and begging for more.

Directions:
In a large bowl, blend together vinegar, lime juice, olive oil, maple syrup, curry powder, cumin, and sea salt. Now add bell pepper, raisins, onion, cilantro and the chickpeas. Blend well. That's it.

PASTA GOODIES SALAD

INGREDIENTS:

6 cups cooked pasta
(use a variety: elbows,
bowties, twists)

½ cup cubed ham

½ cup cubed turkey

½ cup cubed hard salami

½ cup cubed cheddar or
Colby cheese

¼ cup diced celery

¼ cup diced red
bell pepper

Salad dressing (see below)

The amount of dressing
you use is strictly up to you,
whether you like your pasta
salad more wet or more dry.

PASTA GOODIES
SALAD DRESSING

1 ¼ cups mayonnaise

½ cup sugar

2 tablespoons apple cider
vinegar

¼ teaspoon black pepper

1 teaspoon Dijon mustard

Pasta salad is a great addition to a barbecue or picnic, but it can be a little bland. The goodies in this salad make it a hearty side dish. When my daughter, Megan, was young we would induce her to eat green salad by adding lots of extras to the uninteresting bowl of lettuce. Eventually, when offered a salad, Megan would ask, "Is it a goodie salad?" If the answer was yes, she was all in. One day I applied the *goodies* **theory to pasta salad and it became an instant hit.**

Directions:
Cook pasta according to directions on the package. Mix all ingredients in a large bowl. Chill and serve. You can use your favorite bottled dressing, or make your own.

Pasta Goodies Salad Dressing

Directions:
Add all ingredients to a small bowl and blend well. Put a slightly different spin on this salad using your favorite Italian dressing, and sprinkle in some Parmesan cheese.

POTATO SALAD (WITH EGGS AND MUSTARD)

INGREDIENTS:

6-8 medium size potatoes

1 cup mayonnaise

1 tablespoon Dijon mustard

¼ cup dill relish

¼ cup onion (diced)

¼ cup finely diced celery

dill pickle juice
3 hard-boiled eggs
(chopped)

Paprika

THREE GOOD TIPS:

1. Use redskins or Yukon Gold. You don't need to peel those before using.

2. Cool cooked potatoes before you cube them- pieces won't crumble so easily.

3. Don't over mix when you add the dressing. The whole thing will turn to mush.

Potato salad is not complicated, but is a big job when you make a big batch... and when you make potato salad it will likely be for a crowd. This recipe is smaller so that you get the idea. You can build from here.

Directions:

Place potatoes in a large pot with enough water to cover them. Bring to a boil over high heat. Cook 20 to 25 minutes or until potatoes are tender. Allow potatoes to cool (or better yet) refrigerate for several hours. Dice into cubes.

In a bowl combine mayonnaise, mustard, relish, onions, and celery. Add some of the pickle juice to thin the dressing to your liking (probably a couple of tablespoons). Blend well.

Put chopped hard-boiled eggs and cubed potatoes into a large bowl. Gently blend in dressing. Don't over blend and turn your potato salad into potato mush. Sprinkle with paprika, chill and serve.

SUMMER SEAFOOD SALAD

INGREDIENTS:

1 box of Creole or Cajun style rice (Use about 1 cup cooked rice)

1 (8 ounce) package of baby shrimp (cleaned and cooked)

1 (8 ounce) package imitation crabmeat

½ cup diced celery

3 hard-boiled eggs

1 cup mayonnaise

¼ cup sweet relish

2 tablespoons apple cider vinegar

¼ teaspoon black pepper

1 teaspoon Dijon mustard

3 tablespoons water

2 teaspoons sugar

1 teaspoon *The Spice Blend* (See recipe earlier in this book. Or, you can buy a commercial seafood seasoning if you'd rather not make your own).

This is a cool salad for a hot summer day. I use imitation crabmeat in this recipe because it's so much cheaper than the real thing, and disguised among so many other ingredients you really don't notice. If you want to use real crabmeat, that's up to you.

Directions:
Cook rice according to directions on the box. In a small bowl, mix mayonnaise, relish, vinegar, pepper, mustard, water, sugar, and seafood seasoning. Set side. Mince imitation crabmeat in a food processor and place in a large bowl. Add the rice, baby shrimp, celery, and chopped hard-boiled eggs. Blend in dressing.

TACO SALAD

INGREDIENTS:

1 pound ground beef
(or ground turkey)

¼ teaspoon
cayenne pepper

1 teaspoon chili powder

½ teaspoon garlic powder

2 heads of Iceberg lettuce

3 Roma tomatoes (diced)

3 green onion stalks (diced)

½ cup golden corn

1 cup cheddar cheese
(shredded)

1/4 cup chopped
fresh cilantro

1 (16-ounce) bottle Catalina
dressing (or make your own—
see recipe)

1 cup crumbled tortilla chips

CATALINA DRESSING

1 cup ketchup

¼ cup sugar

¼ cup red wine vinegar

¼ cup onion,
(minced very fine)

½ teaspoon paprika

¼ teaspoon
Worcestershire sauce

½ cup Virgin Olive oil

Dash of pepper

Taco Salad is great for a picnic or when you need to bring a dish to share because it travels well. You can mix in the dressing just before serving to keep the lettuce crisp. This recipe serves a crowd. If you don't want to make your own dressing, buy a large bottle of Catalina.

Directions:

In a large pan, brown the ground meat and set aside in a bowl. Sprinkle on cayenne pepper, chili powder, and garlic powder. Mix well. Chop two heads of iceberg lettuce into a large bowl. Add diced tomatoes, green onion, corn, ground meat, shredded cheese, and cilantro. Pour on dressing and toss. Top with crumbled tortilla chips and serve.

Make your own Catalina Dressing

Directions:

Add all ingredients to a small bowl. Blend well and chill.

 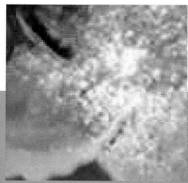 

➤ SAUCES ➤

ALFREDO SAUCE

CREAM BASED

3 tablespoons butter

2 tablespoons olive oil

1 tablespoon minced garlic

2 cups heavy cream

¼ teaspoon pepper (white pepper if you have it)

½ cup grated Parmesan cheese

ROUX BASED

1 tablespoon butter

1 tablespoon flour

1 cup whole milk

1 tablespoon minced garlic

1 tablespoon parsley flakes

1 cup grated Parmesan cheese

Alfredo sauce is a white, creamy sauce most notably served with fettuccine. I've read that a fellow named Alfredo di Lelio (who owned a restaurant in Rome) created the sauce back in 1914. There are two methods of preparation: cream based, and roux based. If you prefer a slightly thicker sauce, start with a roux. I include both recipes here.

Cream Based Alfredo Sauce

Directions:

Melt butter in medium saucepan with olive oil over medium heat. Add garlic, cream, pepper and bring mixture to a simmer. Add the Parmesan cheese and simmer sauce for 8-10 minutes or until sauce has thickened slightly.

Roux Based Alfredo Sauce

Directions:

In a saucepan, bring milk to a simmer over medium heat, stirring occasionally and taking care not to let it boil. The milk should be hot in order to thicken.

In a separate saucepan, heat butter until it melts and becomes frothy. Add garlic. Blend flour into melted butter. Keep folding until you get a smooth golden paste. Slowly add the hot milk to the roux, whisking vigorously to make sure it's free of lumps. When blended smooth, add parsley and Parmesan cheese. Blend in more milk if you want the sauce thinner.

HORSEY SAUCE

INGREDIENTS:

1 cup Mayonnaise

1 tablespoon white vinegar

4 teaspoons sugar

¼ teaspoon salt

2 tablespoons prepared horseradish.

This is a sauce (or spread) that you may not feel is worth the effort of making your own. I usually buy horseradish sauce at the grocery store. But if you don't have any in the fridge, and you don't want to run to the store, it is very easy to whip up your own with ingredients you probably have.

Directions:

Mix all ingredients in a small bowl. Blend thoroughly. Cover container and chill for at least 1 hour.

PRESTO! IT'S PESTO

INGREDIENTS:

2 cups fresh basil leaves (use dry basil if fresh is not available)

½ cup Parmesan cheese

1 teaspoon minced garlic

½ teaspoon salt

½ teaspoon pepper

½ cup toasted pine nuts

1 cups of olive oil

CREAMY PESTO

½ cup pesto

2 cups heavy whipping cream

½ cup Parmesan cheese

¼ teaspoon pepper

Pesto is an Italian sauce that originated in Genoa, Italy. Toss with your favorite pasta instead of red sauce for a little variety. Better yet (just my opinion) is creamy pesto (see below). Or try mixing pesto with mayonnaise for a great sandwich spread. Pesto is so versatile that its uses are limited only by your imagination.

Directions:
Mix all dry ingredients in a food processor until finely blended. Pour in olive oil and blend until smooth.

Creamy Pesto Sauce

Directions:
In a saucepan over medium heat, blend together pesto, heavy cream and Parmesan cheese. Heat until creamy. Do not allow sauce to boil.

RASPBERRY MAPLE CHIPOTLE

INGREDIENTS:

2 tablespoons Olive oil

1 jalapeno pepper (seeded and minced)

1 teaspoon minced garlic

1 (12-ounce) jar of raspberry preserves

½ cup apple cider vinegar

½ teaspoon salt

½ cup brown sugar

¼ cup maple syrup

This is a real nice blend of sweet with tangy. Serve this with Brie or over a block of cream cheese with crackers. Add some Olive oil and you have a salad dressing over spinach. I like it over chicken or grilled salmon.

Directions:

Heat olive oil in a skillet over medium heat. Add diced jalapeno and cook until tender, about 3 minutes. Add garlic and cook one more minute. Add raspberry preserves, apple cider vinegar, salt, and brown sugar. Blend well and simmer until reduced and thickened (about 15 to 20 minutes). Transfer sauce to a bowl and allow it to cool. Now add maple syrup, and it's ready to serve.

REMOULADE

Ingredients:

1 cup mayonnaise

¼ cup chili sauce

½ of a large red pepper
(minced)

½ celery stalk (minced)

2 tablespoons Dijon mustard

1 tablespoon horseradish

1 tablespoon
Worcestershire sauce

Remoulade is another sauce invented by the French. It's sort of like tarter sauce, only more interesting. Remoulade is what Thousand Island dressing hopes to be when it grows up. You won't serve this as a salad dressing, but it is awesome with grilled or blackened chicken or fish… or a dip for chicken nuggets… or a sandwich spread. Most often I serve Remoulade with crab cakes.

Directions:
Mix all ingredients in a food processor until blended and creamy.

SPAGHETTI SAUCE
(JUST LIKE CLEMENZA USED TO MAKE)

INGREDIENTS:

3 tablespoons Canola Oil

½ cup onions (minced)

½ cup green pepper (minced)

1 teaspoon minced garlic

1 (15-ounce) can tomato sauce

1 (28-ounce) can of crushed tomatoes

2 (6-ounce) cans tomato paste (concentrate)

6 (6-ounce) cans of water (use the tomato paste can).

1 teaspoon salt

1 teaspoon dried basil

½ teaspoon red pepper flakes

1 teaspoon oregano

1 teaspoon parsley flakes

¼ cup sugar

¾ cup red wine

(Don't use cheap wine. NEVER cook with wine that you wouldn't drink).

If you don't know who Clemenza is... what are you doing making pasta sauce? Just open a jar, or better yet, a can of Spaghetti O's. So...before we start, go to the Internet and educate yourself. The name is *Peter Clemenza.* **I'll wait.**

If you want to take a break now and watch the *Godfather* **before we start cooking, I completely understand. This would definitely help set the mood. But, if you don't have time right now and want to get right to the cooking, I'm okay with that too. The original recipe came from Director Francis Ford Coppola in honor of his own mother. This is not a copy of that recipe. Taking that would be just the kind of sleazy thing Sollozzo would do for the Tattaglia Family. This is a personal variation based on Clemenza's secret, which is wine and sugar. *Tip: Clemenza mentions to Michael that near the end you** *shove in the sausage and meatballs.* **I prefer to grill sausage. But this is a great recipe to use with** *Mama G's Meatballs* **found in the Main Event section of this book.**

Directions:

Put oil in a sauté pan over medium high heat. When oil is hot, add minced onions and green peppers. Cook for about three minutes, and then add minced garlic. (If you add the garlic too soon, it will burn). When onions and peppers are soft, remove from the sauté pan and set aside.

In a large pot, blend tomato sauce, crushed tomatoes, tomato paste, and water. Stir well and bring to a boil. Reduce heat to a simmer and add salt, basil, oregano, sugar, pepper and onion mixture. Stir in the red wine. Cover (with the lid slightly askew to allow steam to escape) and simmer on low heat for at least two hours. You need to check on it every so often and stir. Make sure the heat is low so it doesn't burn. You want this sauce to reduce down to a fairly thick consistency.

**Bonus Flavor: You don't have to make meatballs with this sauce, but the simmering meatballs add a wonderful bonus flavor. So, if you have time for the extra work of making meatballs, your sauce will be all the better for it. You can find the meatball recipe in the *Main Event* section.

Meat Sauce Variation:

If you want meat sauce but no meatballs: Brown ½ pound ground beef and a ½ pound ground bulk Italian sausage. Put that in the food processor. Add that smooth mix to the tomato sauce to simmer.

Pomodoro Sauce Variation:

You may see this on the menu at your favorite Italian restaurant. I've discovered that Pomodoro sauce is whatever you want it to be. Some describe it as a basic tomato sauce allowed to simmer longer so that it's thicker. More often, Pomodoro sauce is a tomato sauce that is slightly pink and more mellow than traditional red sauce. To accomplish this, add heavy cream to your basic red sauce. It's very nice over pasta. But if you're going with meatballs or Chicken Parmigiana, stick with Clemenza's traditional red sauce.

VODKA SAUCE

INGREDIENTS:

1 teaspoon minced garlic

½ cup onions (minced)

½ cup green pepper (minced)

3 tablespoons Canola Oil

16 ounces tomato sauce

1 28-ounce can of crushed tomatoes

2 (6-ounce) cans of tomato paste (concentrate)

6 (6-ounce) cans of water (use tomato paste can)

1 teaspoons salt

1 teaspoon dried basil

1 teaspoon oregano

¼ cup sugar

¾ cup plain vodka (no flavors)

Heavy whipping cream

In the past fifteen years, vodka sauce has become very popular, even trendy in Italian restaurants. Why? What is the point of putting vodka in spaghetti sauce? To start with, there are really two groups of vodka— plain vodka: colorless and tasteless. Flavored vodka: (cherry, apple, raspberry, vanilla, chocolate). You definitely DO NOT want that in your spaghetti sauce. So, what is the point of adding vodka if it has no taste?

Turns out, there is a point. When cooking tomatoes, alcohol enhances the flavor. Without getting into the science, alcohol causes a chemical reaction that releases additional flavor from tomatoes without adding a new flavor (like when you add red wine). So, adding plain vodka will bring out flavors that would otherwise remain dormant, without contributing an additional flavor to your sauce. The result is that spaghetti sauce prepared with vodka will be slightly more intense, which makes cream the perfect partner to create a mellow pinkish pasta sauce. The recipe here is basically the same as *Clemenza's Secret Pasta Sauce*. **The important difference is that here you replace red wine with vodka, and add heavy cream.**

Directions:

Put 2 tablespoons of oil in a sauté pan over medium high heat. When oil is hot, add minced onions and green peppers. Cook for about three minutes, and then add minced garlic. If you add the garlic too soon, it will burn. When onions and peppers are soft, remove from the sauté pan and set aside.

In a large pot, blend tomato sauce, crushed tomatoes, tomato paste, and water. Stir well and bring to a boil. Reduce heat to a simmer and add salt, basil, oregano, sugar, pepper and onion mixture, and vodka. Simmer at least two hours. You need to check on it every so often and stir. Make sure the heat is low so it doesn't burn. You want this sauce to reduce down to a fairly thick consistency. Blend in the cream until you get to a light pinkish color.

❧ SOUPS ❧

BLACK BEAN SOUP

INGREDIENTS:

1 cup of carrots (diced)

2 tablespoons olive oil

½ cup onion (diced)

½ cup celery (diced)

1 tablespoon minced garlic

4 cups vegetable or
beef broth

1 tablespoon chili powder

1 tablespoon ground cumin

4 (15-ounce) cans
black beans

Fresh cilantro

1 small can whole
kernel corn

I rarely make soup in the summertime. For me, a mug of warm, thick soup goes with autumn leaves or a light snowfall. *Note: If you live in Florida, Arizona, or southern California, disregard that last observation and eat soup whenever you want.

Directions:

Put diced carrots in a pot of boiling water. Cook for 10 minutes. Drain and set aside.

In a large pot, heat oil over medium-high heat. Sauté onion and celery until soft (about three minutes). Add minced garlic for one more minute of cooking. Now add broth, chili powder, cumin, cooked carrots, and three cans of black beans. Bring to a boil. Pour that mixture into a food processor and puree with fresh cilantro. How much cilantro you use is up to your own taste. I use about half of a typical bunch. Blend until smooth. Return that mixture to the large pot. Add remaining can of black beans and corn. Simmer for 15 minutes. Serve with a sprinkle of shredded cheddar cheese on top.

CRABMEAT BISQUE

INGREDIENTS:

2 tablespoons vegetable oil

1 cup carrots (diced)

1 cup onion (diced)

1 tablespoon minced garlic

½ cup celery (diced)

3 medium size tomatoes (diced)

½ cup dry sherry

4 cups seafood stock (if not available- vegetable or chicken stock works fine)

2 tablespoons butter (don't substitute margarine here)

2 tablespoons flour

1 cup heavy cream

1 tablespoon tomato paste

dash cayenne pepper

2 6-oz cans of crabmeat

salt and pepper to taste

Parsley flakes for garnish

How about some bisque trivia? Bisque has become all the rage (tomato bisque, squash bisque, pumpkin bisque). It's all a lie! The truth is that cream soup is only bisque when it contains pureed shellfish, otherwise it's merely cream soup. Aren't you glad you asked? *Tip: The next time you encounter this at a nice restaurant, don't challenge your server on the true nature of bisque. They will only think that you're a loser who spends too much time looking things up on Wikipedia. By the way, in the interest of full disclosure, this recipe calls for both butter and cream so it won't make the top five of the heart-smart list. But once in awhile you have to splurge. Now let's get cooking.

Directions:

In large pot over medium heat, sauté carrots, onion, garlic, and celery in the oil until vegetables are tender. Stir in dry sherry, tomatoes, and vegetable stock. Bring to a rolling boil. Reduce to a simmer, cover, and cook for 15 minutes. Now... pour that mixture into a food processor and puree. When velvety, pour back into the large pot over medium-low heat.

If you've already checked out the section on *Sauces* in this cookbook, then you know all about making a roux. In a small saucepan, melt butter over low heat. Stir in flour and cook until smooth and golden in color. Over medium heat, gradually blend in cream until thick and smooth. Blend that into the tomato puree over medium heat. Stir in tomato paste, cayenne, and crabmeat. Salt and pepper to taste.

MICHIGAN FLIP-TOP CHILI

INGREDIENTS:

1 pound ground
Italian sausage

1 pound ground beef
(or turkey)

1 cup chopped onion

1 cup chopped
green pepper

1 tablespoon minced garlic

2 (16 ounce) cans chili beans

1 (15 ounce) can
tomato sauce

1 (28 ounce) can
diced tomatoes

3 tablespoons chili powder

1 teaspoon dried
parsley flakes

1 teaspoon dried oregano

1 teaspoon ground cumin

1 tablespoon
cayenne pepper

1 tablespoon brown sugar

1 can of beer

The origin of chili is unclear. Some documentation dates back to 16th century Spain. In America, folks in Cincinnati are very proud of their chili... still, chili is generally considered a product of the desert southwest. The Texas legislature designated chili the official state dish in 1977. I'm not going to argue with the whole state of Texas.

This recipe in no way represents authentic Texas chili... the Italian sausage pretty much guarantees that. As for beer, it does for chili what vodka and wine do for pasta sauce. The alcohol unlocks flavors in tomatoes that otherwise remain dormant. Use whatever beer you like (though I'd stay away from anything too thick or bitter). Give me a Bud or a Miller every time. This is Michigan chili— perfect on a cold winter day on the Great Lakes.

Directions:
In a large pot, brown meat with onion, green pepper, and garlic. Blend in all other ingredients. Cover pot and simmer for about 30 minutes.

QUICK CHICKEN SOUP

4 cups water

2 cups carrots (diced)

½ cup onions (minced)

1 cup celery (diced)

4 teaspoons chicken
bouillon granules

48 oz. carton chicken broth

2 cups cooked
chicken (diced)

2 cups uncooked egg
noodles (use more or less
to suit your preference for
noodles)

1 tablespoon parsley flakes

1 teaspoon sage

½ teaspoon *The Spice Blend*
(see recipe)

I know the traditional way to make chicken soup is to start with a raw chicken in boiling water. You cook it for a long time, then pick the bones, and strain the stock that remains. But that's a pain. And then you get this weird gel that forms when the soup has been in the refrigerator. What's up with that anyway? Forget it. I cheat.

First of all, I always have a container of grilled or baked chicken in the refrigerator because we use it in salads, or for a quick snack or a meal. So rather than make this soup the old fashioned way, I recommend using already cooked chicken and a carton of broth. If you're a traditionalist, you'll find lots of recipes on the Internet.

Directions:

Bring water to a boil in a large pot. Add carrots, onions and celery. Cook for about ten minutes. Reduce heat to simmer. Add bouillon granules, broth, cooked chicken, parsley, sage, seasoning spice, and noodles. Simmer for 15 minutes.

SEAFOOD CHOWDER
(THEY'LL NEVER KNOW IT CAME FROM A CAN)

INGREDIENTS:

6 slices of bacon

1 can cream style corn

1 can potato soup
(use ready to serve soup)

1 can clam chowder
(use ready to serve soup)

1 can minced clams
with juice

1 can tiny shrimp

1 can water
chestnuts (sliced)

Dash of Worcestershire sauce

Salt and pepper to taste.

This recipe has three things going for it. It's both elegant and delicious. Your guests will wonder which culinary school you attended. And it takes ten minutes to prepare as long as you know how to open a can.

Directions:

In a large pot, fry bacon until a little crispy. Drain on a paper towel and crumble. Now open the cans. To that same large pot, add the creamed corn, potato soup, clam chowder, minced clams, shrimp, water chestnuts, and Worcestershire sauce. Heat until warm. Serve in small bowls topped with crumbled bacon. Makes about 5 servings.

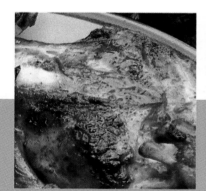

➤ GRILLING ⤶

The first thing to keep in mind is that grilling is a year-round sport. Any day that it's not raining, snowing, or very windy, is a perfect day to fire up the barbecue. I can't share much experience with charcoal grilling since I've used a gas grill for the last twenty years. I love the convenience and ease of a gas grill. And you still get that smoky flavor by using cedar or mesquite chips or planks. But if you're a charcoal griller— no problem. All the same principles apply. But, before we talk about specific foods, let me offer a few tips and tricks about grilling.

Keep it clean.

Always cook on a clean grate. Last week's sausage won't enhance the flavor of this week's ribeye. ***Tip:** Best time to clean the grates is right after the food comes off. You need a bucket of water and a clean rag. Hot grates clean easily.

Careful where you set that dial.

I've had only one real mishap with a gas grill, and that happened twenty-five years ago, though my daughters won't let me forget. I had a gas grill with a glass window just like a real oven. The ribs I was roasting were done... just staying warm. I ran outside and turned the burners from high to very low and ran back into the house to tend to four other dishes also cooking. Fifteen minutes later—Boom! I had inadvertently turned the controls to maximum heat instead of slightly warm. The grill got so hot that the glass window blew out. The inferno reduced my five pounds of ribs to charred nuggets. ***Tip:** Don't get distracted in the kitchen while you have food on the grill outside. Food can burn quickly when ignored too long on the grill.

Where there's smoke, there's flavor.

Don't think for a second that if you have a gas grill, you can't enjoy the added flavor of smoke. Many kinds of wood are available for use on the grill. Use **only** hardwoods such as hickory, oak, cedar, and mesquite. Never use softwoods like pine because they give off resins that infuse food with a weird taste. Soak wood chips or a wood chunk in water for at least 30 minutes before going onto the grill. As the smoke builds, resist the temptation to keep opening the lid.

Grease is the word.

Give the cooking grate a light coating of oil or nonstick cooking spray before you put chicken or steak on the grill. This will help keep food from sticking. I've torn up more than a few chicken breasts because they stuck to the grate.

One good turn DOES NOT deserve another.

Most everything you cook on a grill will need to cook on both sides. But typically, you want to turn meat only once. Turning too often slows cooking and can dry out your food. Most fish and meats should be turned **only once** during cooking.

Back off, Jack!

Fight the urge to start testing for doneness two minutes after you put meat on the grill. This includes opening the lid, poking, moving, turning, and worst of all cutting the meat while it cooks. **Give it a chance to cook.** When the meat is seared on the bottom it pulls away cleanly from the grates when you turn it. If you try to move a boneless chicken breast before it's seared on the bottom, it will definitely stick and tear.

Put the knife away.

For this one, do as I say, not as I do. I think it's a matter of confidence... or lack of it. I never know when a steak is done, so I cut into it to peek inside. This allows all that wonderful juice to escape. Real chefs use the finger test. Poke your steak. A rare steak feels squishy. A medium steak feels springy. A well-done steak feels firm.

What's your hurry?

Here's another tip I got from a professional chef. Don't cut into meat immediately after removing it from the grill because the hot juices will quickly drain away. As the meat cools slightly, the juices thicken and will stay in the meat. So, cover the meat with foil and let it rest for 2-3 minutes. ***Tip:** This does not apply to fish that has very little juice to begin with. You can serve fish immediately.

BOURBON STREET RIBEYE

INGREDIENTS:

THE MARINADE
¼ cup Worcestershire sauce

2 tablespoons light molasses

2 tablespoons Dijon Mustard

¼ cup olive oil

THE RUB
You'll find many rubs available at your favorite grocery store. I like to use the Spice Blend (recipe earlier in this book)

THE GLAZE
¼ cup bourbon

¼ cup Dijon Mustard

¼ cup brown sugar

This recipe turns a good cut of meat into a great one. Once you try this marinade, rub, and glaze… a plain ole steak just won't get it done anymore. The only down side is that you need to plan ahead. This is a two-day process.

First, a couple quick tips about beef. A cheap cut will be dry and tough, and grilling won't improve that. My favorite cut for grilling is a Ribeye. I like steaks that are about an inch thick. A steak thinner than one inch can dry out pretty quickly. And don't trim your steak too lean before cooking. A little fat adds flavor (and smoke).

*Tip: Beef tenderloin cooks better when it's closer to room temperature. Never take a steak right out of the refrigerator and put it on the grill. Let your raw steak sit for at least thirty minutes before you cook. No worries about bacteria from sitting for such a short time. Now, let's get to the cooking.

Directions:
Make the marinade: In a small bowl, blend the Worcestershire sauce, molasses, Dijon mustard, and olive oil. Place your steaks in a large zip-lock bag. Pour marinade over the steaks. Push out all of the air. Seal the bag and put it in a bowl and into the refrigerator overnight.

Time to cook:
Remove steaks from the marinade and wipe clean with your hands. Don't rinse the steaks with water. Discard the marinade. Apply the rub mix onto both sides of your steaks.. Set them aside for thirty minutes. Fire up the grill.

Make the glaze: Mix together the bourbon, Dijon mustard and brown sugar until sugar is dissolved. Set the glaze aside and put those steaks on the grill.

When time comes to turn your steak over on the grill, **don't use a fork**. When you pierce the meat you lose a lot of delicious juice. Use tongs. Just before you turn brush on some of the glaze.

To test for doneness, use the push test. Poke the steak with a finger. A rare steak feels squishy. A medium steak feels springy. A well-done steak feels firm. Most important, **do not** cut into the steak while it's on the grill. You'll lose the juice, and the steak will dry out. If you want to cook a 1-inch thick Ribeye by the clock, rare takes approximately 5-7 minutes. Medium: 8-10 minutes. Well done: 10-12 minutes. Turn your steaks halfway through the cooking time. About two minutes before taking your steaks off the grill, brush with more glaze.

Remember, steak will continue to cook after you take it off the grill, so slightly undercook the meat to get the results you or your guests want. After you take the steaks off the grill, let them sit for 2-3 minutes on a plate wrapped loosely in foil. This allows juices to thicken and absorb back into the meat.

CHICKEN ON THE BARBIE

Grilled chicken is awesome! Unless it's horrible! It's pretty easy to end up on either side of the street. Your success with barbecued chicken is about 20% spice and sauce, and 80% cooking. I recommend a combination of grill and oven. The number one area of concern is your health. Most raw chicken you buy carries bacteria that can make your family or your guests sick. The good news is that sufficient cooking kills harmful bacteria. Let's look at cooking options.

CHICKEN ON THE GRILL (USING ONLY THE GRILL)

I know many fine cooks who put raw chicken pieces directly on the grill, and do just fine with that cooking method. But it's easy to make a mistake. Often the outside of chicken breasts and thighs gets charred and crispy while the inside remains undercooked. This brings two results: Everyone gets sick. And your guests resemble hyenas in a National Geographic special tearing at the carcass of a gazelle. Yuk!

Grill and Oven Combination

Many people will tell you this is backwards, that you should bake first and finish on the grill, but I think this method gives you more control and less mess.

Directions:

Preheat oven to 300°. Preheat grill to get it nice and hot (450°-500°). Wash chicken pieces. Sprinkle with seasoning. I often use a premixed seasoning from the store (mesquite, hickory, or any smoky flavor). I sometimes use The Spice Blend.

Spray non-stick spray, or brush a little oil on the grates to keep the chicken from stickin'. Put chicken pieces on the grill and let them sizzle and smoke for ten minutes. Don't open the lid. Leave them alone. This will put nice grill marks on the skin and infuse smoky flavor. Turn them over and cook ten more minutes.

Remove chicken from grill and spread pieces out in a baking dish. Add ¼ cup of water to the dish and brush chicken generously with barbecue sauce. Cover tightly with foil and bake for 90 minutes.

Most people will argue that's too long and the chicken will dry out. It's not. And it won't. Remove from oven and allow pan to rest for ten minutes while chicken soaks all that juice back in. Baste again with Barbecue sauce, and you're ready to serve.

SMOKIN' GOOD RIBS

INGREDIENTS:

1 or 2 racks of baby back ribs

Rib rub (see recipe below)

Barbecue Sauce

Large roasting pan

Hickory or Mesquite Wood chips (soaking in a pan of water for the grill)

Aluminum foil

RIB RUB

½ cup brown sugar

¼ cup paprika

1 tablespoon basil

1 tablespoon black pepper

1 tablespoon salt

1 tablespoon chili powder

1 tablespoon garlic powder

1 tablespoon onion powder

1 teaspoon cayenne

Mix all ingredients in a small bowl.

When it's summertime…(or spring, autumn, or winter) it's a good time for ribs. But you have a choice to make: Spareribs or baby back ribs? Let's start with a test of your ribs IQ. There is a difference between spareribs and baby back ribs. Spareribs are cut from the belly of a pig (where bacon comes from). They are meatier and bigger. But bigger is not always better.

Baby Back ribs are cut from the loin section (where pork chops come from) and are smaller, less fatty, and more tender than spareribs. The rack tapers from long to short. The shortest bones are typically about 3 inches, and the longest is usually about 6 inches. A typical rack has 10-13 bones. Baby back ribs are, by far, the more popular choice.

Don't be afraid…

Many people avoid cooking ribs because they think it requires lots of attention and technique. Okay, properly prepared baby back ribs do require lots of time, attention and technique. But it's worth it.

If you don't have access to a grill, you can roast ribs using only your oven, though it's hard to get that real smoky flavor. You can also use only your grill. The challenge there is controlling the heat. I believe you'll get best results using a combination of grill and oven. And most important— you have to be patient. The key is slow roasting.

Directions:
(It all starts with the rub.)

The *rub* is the dry mixture that you rub onto the ribs before roasting. Like barbecue sauce, you will find a variety of styles (Kansas City, St. Louis, Carolina, Texas, Memphis). This recipe is *Detroit Style*.

Rib Rub
Directions:
Prepare the rack of ribs:

First, remove the skin. This is the membrane on the back of the ribs that doesn't look like much, but gets tough when you roast. You can usually get a fingernail under the edge, grip with paper towel and pull it off. If you have to, use a knife to trim it away.

*Tip: If it seems impossible to get the membrane off, it may already gone. Some prepackaged ribs have the skin already removed. Lucky you! Rinse the rack and pat dry. Now apply the rub to both sides. Wrap the rack in foil or plastic and put in the refrigerator for at least two hours, or overnight if you have planned ahead.

Time to roast those ribs!

Pre-heat your oven to 275°. Fire up the grill and get it hot. If the ribs are for dinner... you need to start cooking before lunch.

Start on the grill. Put some wet wood chips on a piece of foil directly over the heat on the grill. Remove the ribs from foil and grill for ten minutes. Don't open the lid to check on them. They're fine. Turn the rack over and grill ten more minutes. Keep the lid closed as much as possible to let them soak in that smoke.

Now, the ribs go into the oven. Place the ribs in a roasting pan. Add about a cup of water to the pan. Baste ribs with barbecue sauce. Cover with foil and roast for three hours. When three hours have passed... turn the ribs over, baste with barbecue sauce again. Add water if necessary so pan doesn't dry out. Cover with foil and bake another two hours. Baste with more sauce and serve. Experiment to find just the right timing. Patience with a slow roast is always the key.

SALMON ON THE GRILL

I'm a big fan of salmon. I like it best grilled which works out well since my wife doesn't allow me to cook fish in the house. That's okay because the grill is the best place for salmon. I grill salmon three different ways: Blackened, cedar plank, or foil wrapped.

BLACKENED SALMON

To me, a work of art is a seasoned salmon fillet sizzling on a hot cast iron skillet. I could be wrong about the origin, but I believe chef Paul Prudhomme popularized if not invented this technique most often associated with Cajun cuisine. You need a cast iron pan or griddle, which you won't use for a lot of things, but the pan is relatively inexpensive and it's worth it.

You also need blackening spice. You can buy a pre-made jar at the grocery store, but don't do it. You'll spend four dollars for 30-cents worth of spices that you already have in your pantry.

Directions:
Mix all ingredients in a bowl. Pour mixture into a jar that you can seal tight.

Cooking Instructions:
Fire up the grill! You want the grill very hot. Put your cast iron pan in the barbecue to heat up.

While the skillet heats up, prepare the fish. Rinse thoroughly. Sprinkle a fairly generous amount of blackening spice on the fleshy side of the fillet. Cut the fillet into serving size pieces. You can probably fit two pieces on the skillet at the same time. At the grill, spread a tablespoon or two of Canola oil on the hot pan. Place the fish on the pan *seasoned side down*. Close the lid and let it cook for about five minutes. Turn the fillet(s) over, cook for another 3-5 minutes. That's it.

CEDAR PLANK SALMON

If you want to make your neighbors jealous, fill the air with the fragrance of a smoking cedar plank on your grill. This is a very simple but elegant way to prepare and serve salmon. Unlike blackened salmon with a slightly crisp texture, plank salmon bakes which leaves the fish more tender. Add to that the woodsy cedar flavor from the smoking plank and this is hard to beat.

First the planks:

You can find cedar planks at most any store that sells grills and barbecue *supplies,* or a many outlets online. They're relatively inexpensive *and* can be re-used. Prepare the plank by soaking it for at least one hour in a bucket or pan of water. This prevents the plank from burning on the grill. Try adding one cup of apple juice or white wine to the water to give the wood a fruity accent.

Prepare the salmon:

This part is the same as blackened salmon. Rinse the fillet thoroughly. Now, sprinkle some of the blackening spice on the fleshy side of the fillet. Place the fish on the plank (seasoned side up.)

On the grill:

Get your grill good and hot. Resist the temptation to open the lid to check on the salmon. You want to keep all that delightful cedar smoke inside. Start checking salmon for doneness after about 10 minutes. The salmon is done when you push on it and it is firm. ***Tip:** Planked food does not need to be turned during grilling. Cook for about 15-minutes total.

Reusing your plank:

Rinse a used plank with soap and water and let it dry. Store plank in a dry, clean place and simply re-soak it the next time. You can probably get two uses out of a plank, then crumble up the charred plank to use as smoking chips.

Fast and Easy Foil Wrapped Salmon

As the name suggests, this method requires the least amount of preparation. It's still delicious but lacks the crunch of blackened and the smoky flavor of planked salmon. But sometimes I just want to do things the easy way.

Heat your grill to about 400° or a medium heat-setting. Rinse the salmon fillet, and sprinkle blackening spice on the fleshy side of the fillet. Tear off a long piece of aluminum foil and coat it lightly with some non-stick spray. Place the entire fillet seasoned side up on the foil. Tear off a second sheet of foil and spray it. Lay it over the fillet and crimp the two sheets of foil together on all sides. Grill for about 15 minutes.

⤜ THE MAIN EVENT ⤛

BEEF STROGANOFF

INGREDIENTS:

1 pound beef tenderloin

6 tablespoons
butter or margarine

½ pound (about 2 ½ cups)
sliced fresh mushrooms

½ cup diced onion

1 can beef broth

2 tablespoons ketchup

1 teaspoon minced garlic

1 teaspoon salt

2 tablespoons flour

1 teaspoon
Worcestershire sauce

¼ cup dry red wine

1 cup sour cream

3 to 4 cups of cooked wide
flat noodles

When you want to prepare a meal that speaks elegance, sensuality, even romance... Italian cuisine wins. But, Beef Stroganoff served over warm buttered noodles is a close second. *Tip: A common mistake is to select a poor cut of meat thinking it will simmer like stew and tenderize. Don't ruin a beautiful stroganoff by saving a few dollars at the meat counter. You're only buying a pound. Invest in a good cut of beef.

Directions:

Remove meat from its packaging. Rinse. Pat dry and place in the freezer for ten to fifteen minutes. You will want meat sliced fairly thin, and it will slice much more easily if slightly frozen. While you wait... In a large Dutch oven or large saucepan melt 2 tablespoons of margarine and sauté the mushrooms, onion and garlic until tender. Remove from pan and set aside. Now slice the meat into pieces that are about an inch long and maybe a ¼ inch thick. In the same pan you already used, melt 2 tablespoons of margarine and brown the meat. Remove meat from pan and set aside in a bowl.

In the same pan melt 2 tablespoons of margarine and blend in the flour. Add the broth and cook until that begins to thicken. Recognize this? Velouté! Add the browned meat, onion/mushroom mixture, Worcestershire sauce, and red wine. Heat to boiling; reduce heat. Cover and simmer 20 minutes. Remove from heat and stir in sour cream. Serve over warm noodles.

CHICKEN MARSALA (SORT OF)

INGREDIENTS:

3 chicken breasts
(boneless and skinless)

¾ cup flour
(for dredging chicken)

¼ teaspoon thyme

¼ teaspoon sage

½ teaspoon black pepper

½ teaspoon paprika

¼ cup olive oil

2 tablespoons butter
(or margarine)

1 medium onion diced

2 cups sliced fresh
mushrooms

1 teaspoon minced garlic

½ cup white wine
(or Marsala)

¾ cup chicken broth

This is a very elegant dish that will have your guests thinking you spent hours in the kitchen. Don't tell the secret that this one takes 30 minutes or less prep and cooking time.

*Tip: The most common mistake here is choosing a cheap wine under the false assumption that it doesn't matter since when used in cooking the flavor is disguised. A chef once told me, "Never cook with wine that you wouldn't drink." And of course, he's right. You can get a perfectly delicious wine for under $15. It's worth it. I call this *Chicken Marsala (sort of)* because I usually make it with white wine not Marsala. My wife prefers white wine, and I like the clear color of the sauce. If you prepare real Chicken Marsala, you need to use Marsala wine.

A little bit about wine— Marsala wine is Italy's most famous fortified wine. What, you ask, is a fortified wine? That means distilled liquor, like brandy, is added to boost the alcohol content up to about 20 percent. Marsala is not a red wine, but usually a more golden color. Okay, let's get to the cooking.

Directions:

In a bowl, combine flour, thyme, sage, black pepper, and paprika. Stir to combine. Slice the boneless chicken breasts into ½ inch thick slices. I suggest the same technique as with slicing raw beef. Remove the meat from packaging, rinse, and put in the freezer for about fifteen minutes to make slicing easier. Next you dredge the chicken pieces in the flour mixture. Dredging simply means dunk each piece in the flour mixture, coat it, shake off the excess, and set it aside. Heat oil in a sauté pan. Add chicken pieces and cook for about four minutes (2 minutes on each side). Remove chicken from the pan and set aside. In that same pan, add 2 tablespoons of butter to the already hot oil. When melted, cook the onions, mushrooms, and garlic for about two minutes scraping the pan as you cook. Add the chicken back into the pan. Add wine. Cook until the sauce has slightly thickened. Now add the chicken broth. Cover and simmer for about ten minutes. Chicken Marsala goes well over brown rice or angel hair pasta.

CHICKEN PARMESAN (PARMIGIANA)

INGREDIENTS:

4 boneless chicken breasts.

2 eggs

½ cup milk

Italian seasoned breadcrumbs

½ cup Canola oil

1 package sliced Mozzarella cheese

1 jar (16 oz) spaghetti sauce (or better yet, make your own— see recipe)

Parmesan cheese

Food prepared *parmigiana* is a staple of an Italian menu. The most common meats used are veal and chicken. The only vegetable parmigiana I know of is eggplant, which has a slightly different recipe (also in this book).

Directions:

I recommend you pound the chicken breasts (½ to ¾ of an inch thickness). To do this, put a breast in a plastic storage bag (or between two sheets of plastic wrap). Pound the breast with a kitchen hammer (if you have one) or a rolling pin.

In a bowl, whisk together the eggs and milk. Put about two cups of breadcrumbs in a separate bowl. Dip chicken breasts in milk and egg mixture and then in breadcrumbs. Coat both sides.

Heat a large skillet over medium-high heat. Add oil. When the oil is hot enough to sauté, place chicken in skillet and fry to a golden brown (about 2 minutes on each side.) Spoon a light layer of sauce into a baking dish and add the chicken breasts. Spoon a little sauce over each chicken breast. Cover dish with foil and bake at 350° for about 25 minutes. Remove foil. Top each chicken breast with a slice of mozzarella cheese and bake uncovered five more minutes. Serve with spaghetti, garlic bread and a Caesar Salad. Manja Bene!

CINCINNATI CHILI

INGREDIENTS:

1 medium onion
finely chopped

1 pound extra-lean
ground beef

1 teaspoon minced garlic

2 tablespoons chili powder

1 teaspoon ground allspice

2 teaspoons ground
cinnamon

1 teaspoon ground cumin

½ teaspoon red
(cayenne) pepper

½ teaspoon salt

2 tablespoons
unsweetened cocoa

1 (15-ounce)
can tomato sauce

1 tablespoon
Worcestershire sauce

1 tablespoon cider vinegar

1 cup beef broth

½ cup water

1 (16-ounce) package
of spaghetti

Maybe I've lived a sheltered life, but until a few years ago, I had never heard of putting chili on top of spaghetti. Little did I realize that it's a long and loved tradition in Cincinnati. Folks there consider their city the chili capital of the world, though I suspect you'd get an argument from the good people of Texas. But, Cincinnati-style chili is quite different. Their chili is thinner and prepared with cinnamon, cocoa, and Worcestershire sauce— then served over spaghetti. Yeah, I was pretty skeptical too.

Directions:

In a large frying pan over medium-high heat, sauté onion, ground beef, garlic, and chili powder until ground beef is slightly cooked. Add allspice, cinnamon, cumin, cayenne pepper, salt, unsweetened cocoa, tomato sauce, Worcestershire sauce, cider vinegar, beef broth, and water. Reduce heat to low and simmer uncovered for one hour. Turn off heat and cover. Cook spaghetti according to package directions. Ladle Cincinnati Chili mixture over the cooked spaghetti and serve. Here's where you offer the authentic touch.

Served *3-Way*: Chili and spaghetti— topped with shredded cheddar cheese.

Served *4-Way*: Chili and spaghetti— topped with cheddar cheese and raw onions.

Served *5-Way*: Chili and spaghetti— topped with cheddar, onions and kidney beans.

CRAB CAKES

INGREDIENTS:

1 (6-ounce) can of crabmeat

1 (8-ounce) package of imitation crabmeat (minced into flakes)

½ cup breadcrumbs

¼ cup finely minced red bell pepper

¼ cup minced onions

¼ cup mayonnaise

1 egg

1 teaspoon Worcestershire sauce

1 teaspoon Poupon mustard

1 tablespoon lemon juice

1 teaspoon parsley flakes

1 tablespoon The Spice Blend (See recipe)

1 cup Canola oil

Crab cakes make a great appetizer, or a stand-alone entrée. I cheat a little on the recipe and substitute imitation crabmeat for part of the amount because real crabmeat gets very expensive. But if you want authentic crab cakes, you have to splurge and buy real crab meat. The key to good crab cakes is to go as light as possible on the breadcrumbs. I serve them with the Remoulade sauce (see recipe).

Directions:

Pre-heat oven to 350°. Combine crabmeat in a bowl. Add breadcrumbs, bell pepper, onion, mayonnaise, egg, Worcestershire sauce, mustard, lemon juice, parsley flakes and seasoning. Mix well. Form mixture into patties. It's your call on how large or small you want to make them. Arrange patties on a plate and put the plate in the freezer for fifteen minutes. This will help hold them together when you sauté. Heat a pan and add oil until hot. Sauté crab cakes about two minutes on each side. You want a nice golden brown, but don't overdo it. I usually make mine thick (as in the photo) so I arrange the crab cakes on a cookie sheet and bake for ten minutes in a 350° oven. Serve with Remoulade sauce.

CAVATAPPI SALSICCIA

INGREDIENTS:

1 package Cavatappi
(corkscrew pasta)

1 pound ground
Italian sausage

3 tablespoons butter

1 teaspoon minced garlic

2 cups heavy
whipping cream

1 cup Parmesan cheese

1 tablespoon Rosemary

½ teaspoon crushed
red pepper

¼ teaspoon pepper

1 cup cooked peas

I first had this dish at an Italian restaurant in Ann Arbor, Michigan (which if you have never visited is an awesome town.) I didn't ask for the recipe since I knew the chef wouldn't give up the goods, but I made notes and came up with this. The pasta I use is called Cavatappi, also known as celentani, amori, spirali, or tortiglioni. Cavatappi is an Italian word that means corkscrew... which is the label you may find on the box at the grocery store. Salsiccia means sausage in Italian. By the way, if you want to bore your friends with useless knowledge: This pasta is technically macaroni. The general term macaroni is any pasta cut into tubes.

Directions:

Boil the Cavatappi as directed on package and set aside in a bowl of cool water. Brown ground Italian sausage and set aside. In a small pan, melt butter. Cook minced garlic for about two minutes. Add cream, Parmesan cheese, and pepper. Cook over medium heat until blended smooth. In a large pot, combine pasta with cream mixture. Add rosemary, crushed red pepper, ground sausage and peas. Pour into a large serving bowl. Sprinkle with Parmesan cheese.

EGGPLANT PARMESAN
(PARMIGIANA)

INGREDIENTS:

2 large eggplants
(trimmed at both ends)

1 package of fry batter mix

1 cup Canola oil

16-ounce package shredded
Mozzarella cheese

1 jar (16 oz) spaghetti sauce
(or better yet, make your
own— see recipe)

Parmesan cheese

Eggplant parmigiana is probably my very favorite dish. It's gooey and cheesy and serves as a main dish or a side. For Chicken Parmigiana I use breadcrumbs... but for eggplant, I suggest you use frying batter instead. I think you'll like the slight difference in texture.

Directions:

Pre-heat oven to 350°. In a bowl, prepare a thin batter following package directions. Slice the eggplants into ¼ inch thick discs. Heat a large skillet over medium-high heat. Add oil. When oil is hot enough to sauté, dip a slice of eggplant into the batter. Let it drip to a thin coating and place the battered slice into the oil. Cook for about one minute on each side. If you use a large skillet, you can probably cook four or five slices at the same time. When golden brown, remove slices to a plate until the whole batch is done. Spoon a thin layer of sauce into a 9x13 baking dish. Add a layer of eggplant, and then a layer of cheese. Repeat the pattern: sauce, eggplant, cheese until you run out of room. Finish with a layer of sauce. Cover with foil and bake for 35 minutes. Remove foil. Top dish with layer of Mozzarella cheese and bake for ten more minutes until cheese is gooey. Sprinkle with Parmesan cheese and serve.

LASAGNA

SAUCE
1 pound ground beef

1 pound ground lean pork

1 teaspoon minced garlic

½ cup onions (minced)

2 tablespoons Canola Oil

1 (16-ounce) can of tomato sauce

1 (8-ounce) can of tomato paste (concentrate)

5 cups of water

1 teaspoon salt

1 teaspoon dried basil

1 teaspoon oregano

2 tablespoons sugar

2 tablespoons parsley

3/4 cup red wine (Don't use cheap wine)

CHEESE FILLING
2 (12oz.) cartons cottage cheese

1 (12oz.) carton ricotta cheese

2 eggs

½ cup Parmesan cheese

1 tablespoon parsley flakes

1 ½ teaspoons salt

1 teaspoon oregano

BULDING THE LASAGNA
1 pound package Mozzarella cheese (shredded or slices)

1 package lasagna noodles (cooked as directed on box)

Sauce Mixture

Cheese Mixture

If you're Italian, nobody makes lasagna like your mom. My mom is German, but that's beside the point. She makes great lasagna! My dad is 100% Italian, but the extent of his cooking expertise is a recipe for cornflakes: Put flakes in bowl. Add milk. Eat cornflakes. So, the job of maintaining the Italian portion of our heritage fell to mom. The only mistake I occasionally make is not allowing the sauce to cook down long enough. You need to simmer a lot of the water out of the sauce, or your finished lasagna will be watery. You want that sauce thick when you start building the layers.

Directions:

Put 2 tablespoons of oil in a sauté pan over medium high heat. When oil is hot, add ground beef and pork, minced onions, and green peppers. When meat is nearly browned, add minced garlic. If you add the garlic too soon, it will burn. Completely brown meat mixture, then run it through the food processor (if you have one).

In a large pot, blend tomato sauce, tomato paste, and water. Stir well and bring to a boil. Reduce heat to a simmer and add salt, basil, oregano, sugar, parsley, pepper, meat mixture, and the red wine. Cover and simmer for about two hours. You need to check on it every so often and stir. **Make sure the heat is low so it doesn't burn**. You want this sauce to reduce to a thick consistency.

Cheese Filling
Directions:
Mix all ingredients in a bowl.

Building the Lasagna:
Directions:
Heat oven to 375°. In a 13x9 baking dish start building your layers:

1. Meat sauce

2. Noodles

3. Ricotta cheese mixture

4. Mozzarella cheese

5. Repeat.

Finish off with a final layer of noodles and cover with a light coating of sauce (to keep the noodles from getting too crisp as the lasagna bakes. Cover with foil and bake 30 minutes. Uncover and bake another 20 minutes. Let the pan cool for ten minutes. Sprinkle with parmesan cheese and serve.

MAMA G'S MEATBALLS

INGREDIENTS:

1 pound lean ground beef

1 pound ground
Italian sausage

1 cup Italian seasoned
bread crumbs

½ cup of milk

2 eggs, beaten

½ cup Parmesan cheese

½ cup onions (minced)

1 tablespoon mustard

1 tablespoon dried parsley

1 teaspoon garlic salt

1 tablespoon
Worcestershire sauce

1 cup Canola Oil
(for browning meatballs)

Spaghetti and meatballs doesn't have the elegance of Chicken Marsala, but it's a great meal for your family or a large crowd. Kids big and small love spaghetti and meatballs. This is the time to put on some Lou Monte, and break out the checkered tablecloths and Chianti. Wait a minute… first I find out you don't know Peter Clemenza, now I get the feeling you don't know Lou Monte. Don't even start this recipe until you download *Luna Mezzo Mare.*

The Sauce

For the sauce, prepare *Just Like Clemenza's Secret Pasta Sauce*. There's no need to reprint the recipe here. If you don't want to make sauce from scratch, buy three large jars of your favorite spaghetti sauce and heat in a large pot. Add ½ cup of red wine. The meatballs will simmer in the sauce later.

The Meatballs

Directions:

Your sauce should be simmering on the stove before you start the meatballs.

Combine all of the ingredients **except the oil** in a large mixing bowl. Using your hands, mix well. Chill mixture 15 to 20 minutes. Now comes the part where you put on the music, because this takes awhile. Roll the meat mixture between your palms into golf-ball-size balls. Set them aside as you roll.

In a large frying pan, heat 1 cup of oil. When oil is hot, add 6 or 8 meatballs. Turn the meatballs frequently to brown all sides. ***Tip:** Fry the meatballs only long enough to brown. The meatballs will finish cooking in the sauce.

When first batch is browned, remove and drain on a paper towel. Add another batch of meatballs to the frying pan to brown. Continue this process until all meatballs are browned. Add them to the pot of sauce to simmer for at least 30 minutes.

MANICOTTI VS. CANNELLONI

MANICOTTI CREPES
1 cup all purpose flour

2 eggs

½ cup of milk

½ cup water

¼ teaspoon salt

2 tablespoons of
butter (melted)

RICOTTA CHEESE FILLING
2 cups ricotta cheese

2 cups cottage cheese

1 cup cooked
chopped spinach

1 egg

¼ cup grated
Parmesan cheese

2 tablespoons chopped
fresh parsley

½ teaspoon salt

¼ teaspoon ground
black pepper

This is not a big deal, but it bothers me that people interchange the words manicotti and cannelloni. They are not the same thing. Just so you know: Traditional manicotti is made with a crepe, which is a very thin pancake. I'm not sure if the French invented the crepe, but Italians have put it to good use. Traditional manicotti has a ricotta filling. As for sauce: I recommend a béchamel (white sauce). Crepes are delicate and so is the sauce. But if you want to use a red sauce, that's perfectly fine.

Cannelloni is made with a tube-shaped pasta that is usually boiled, and then stuffed and baked. The filling is typically ricotta or meat. Use a red sauce for cannelloni. You can make your own spaghetti sauce (see recipe in this book), or open a jar. The same goes for the white sauce. If you don't want to make your own, substitute a jar of Alfredo sauce. Okay? Let's go!

Cannelloni Tubes

If you want to make cannelloni you generally have to buy manicotti. You heard me. The box of pasta tubes you find at the grocery store will almost always say manicotti. Don't explain the difference to the store manager because he doesn't care. Just buy the pasta tubes and revel in the knowledge that you know the truth.

Manicotti Crepes

Directions to make crepes:
In large mixing bowl, whisk flour and eggs. Gradually add milk and water stirring to combine. Add salt, butter, and beat until smooth. Heat (to medium high) a small, lightly oiled sauté pan (non-stick surface). Pour approximately ¼ cup of batter into the pan. Tilt pan with circular motion so that batter coats surface evenly. Flip the crepe after about 1 minute. Cook 30 seconds more. Crepes take practice. Be patient.

Ricotta Cheese Filling

Directions:
Mix all ingredients in a large bowl.

INGREDIENTS:

MEAT FILLING

1 lb. ground Italian sausage

1 pound ground beef

½ cup onions

1 tablespoon minced garlic

2 tablespoons canola oil

¼ cup cooked chopped spinach

½ cup grated Parmesan cheese

2 tablespoons chopped parsley

1 tablespoon oregano

½ teaspoon salt

¼ teaspoon ground black pepper

Meat Filling

Directions:

In a sauté pan, brown sausage and ground beef. Set aside. Add 2 tablespoons of oil to the same pan and brown the onions (approximately 3 minutes). Add garlic for the final minute of cooking. If garlic cooks too long it will burn.

Combine meat and onions in food processor to make a smooth consistency.

In a large bowl combine, meat mixture, spinach, Parmesan cheese, parsley, oregano, salt, and pepper.

Putting It All Together

Preheat oven to 350°. If you're making manicotti, spoon some Béchamel sauce onto bottom of a baking dish. Now, spoon a generous amount of ricotta filling onto a crepe and roll into a tube. Place tubes carefully in the dish. Cover with foil and bake for about 25 minutes. Spoon more sauce over each manicotti and serve. Again, if you prefer red sauce, go for it. You're the chef here. Do what you like.

For cannelloni, stuff a pasta tube with filling. Spoon a layer of sauce onto the bottom of a baking dish. Lay out tubes in the dish. Spoon some sauce over each tube. Sprinkle with Parmesan cheese. Cover the dish with foil and bake for about 20 minutes. Remove foil and bake ten more minutes. Spoon more sauce over each tube and serve.

Manicotti

vs.

Cannelloni

MEAT LOAF JUST LIKE JUNE CLEEVER USED TO MAKE

INGREDIENTS:

2 pounds ground beef

2 eggs slightly beaten

1 cup milk

1 cup breadcrumbs

½ cup Parmesan cheese

1 tablespoon Worcestershire sauce

1 tablespoon parsley flakes

½ teaspoon garlic powder

½ cup onions (finely chopped)

2 tablespoons ketchup

1 can of beef gravy (or spaghetti sauce, or seasoned diced tomatoes)

It's quite possible that you don't know who June Cleever is, and have never had meatloaf. Ahhh… you've missed so much. For me, it's a trip down memory lane with chicken pot pies and TV dinners. Growing up, we had meatloaf once a week, with mashed potatoes and peas. The recipe is pretty basic. Your choices come with picking a sauce (beef gravy, spaghetti sauce, or maybe stewed tomatoes). It's your call.

Directions:

Preheat oven to 350°. Thoroughly mix all ingredients except the gravy. Form into a loaf and place in a 13 x 9 inch baking dish. Add a ¼ cup of water to the pan and bake for 50 minutes. Pour gravy, sauce, or tomatoes over the loaf and bake ten more minutes. Allow the meatloaf to stand for 5 minutes before slicing.

If you decide that you like meatloaf, get creative with the sauce. Try sweet and sour sauce, or teriyaki. Add your favorite barbecue sauce to the brown gravy. Experiment a little. That's the fun in cooking.

RISOTTO
(WITH INGREDIENT WHOSE NAME SHALL NOT BE SPOKEN)

INGREDIENTS:

6 cups chicken broth

¼ cup margarine

2 tablespoons Canola Oil

6 slices bacon (cut into small pieces)

3 tablespoons oil

1 cup diced onions

1 container chicken liver (no more than 20 ounces)

½ teaspoon salt

½ teaspoon pepper

3 cups uncooked white rice

1 tablespoon ground saffron (use more or less to your taste)

1 cup chopped fresh mushrooms (or a small can of mushrooms pieces)

I don't make Risotto very often because this is my mom's signature dish, and mine is never as good. But then, nothing you make is going to taste as good as when your mom made it. But give it a shot. Warning: When you read the ingredients, don't just say *blech* and move on to the next recipe. Keep an open mind. Yes, this Risotto dish contains chicken livers, and that will scare off a lot of people. Try it. I think you'll like it. But don't surprise your guests with this. Someone will ask, "Say, what is the meat in this dish?" When you answer, "Chicken liver," a stunned hush will fall over the dining room. If you do give it a try (and I hope you will) risotto stands alone as an entrée and goes perfectly with a Caesar salad, garlic bread, and your favorite red wine.

Directions:

Pour broth into a pot and bring to a boil. Place margarine and oil in a Dutch oven or very large pot over medium heat. When hot, add bacon and cook until slightly brown. Add onions and mushrooms for an additional two or three minutes. Before adding the chicken livers, dice the bacon into small pieces. Now add the liver and cook until brown. Cut the liver into small pieces as it cooks. Add rice and mix well. Cook for about 3 minutes. Now pour in the broth. Stir well, cover, and simmer until rice is done, about 25 minutes. Add saffron and blend well. If rice seems dry, add more broth to your liking. Sprinkle with Parmesan cheese and serve.

STUFFED SHELLS

INGREDIENTS:

RICOTTA CHEESE FILLING
2 cups ricotta cheese

2 cups cottage cheese

1 cup cooked chopped spinach

1 egg

¼ cup grated
Parmesan cheese

2 tablespoons chopped
fresh parsley

½ teaspoon salt

¼ teaspoon ground black pepper

Directions: Mix all ingredients
in a large bowl

MEAT FILLING
1 lb. ground Italian sausage

1 pound ground beef

½ cup onions

1 tablespoon minced garlic

2 tablespoons canola oil

¼ cup cooked
chopped spinach

½ cup grated
Parmesan cheese

2 tablespoons chopped parsley

1 tablespoon oregano

½ teaspoon salt

¼ teaspoon ground black pepper

If you've already made manicotti or cannelloni, then you will recognize that stuffed shells are the same thing only different. You need spaghetti sauce (homemade or a jar). You need pasta shells, which you buy at the grocery store. And you will choose a filling.

The Shells: Prepare as directed on package. Set aside in a large bowl of cool water.

Directions:

In a sauté pan, brown sausage and ground beef. Set aside in a bowl. Add 2 tablespoons of oil to the same pan and brown the onions approximately 3 minutes. Add garlic for the final minute of cooking. If garlic cooks too long it will burn. Combine meat and onions in food processor to make a smooth consistency. In a large bowl combine, meat, spinach, Parmesan cheese, parsley, oregano, salt, and pepper.

Baking the Shells

Preheat oven to 350°. Spoon a layer of sauce into a baking dish. Stuff the cooked shells and spread them out in the dish. Sprinkle with Parmesan cheese. Cover the dish with foil and bake for about 25 minutes.

 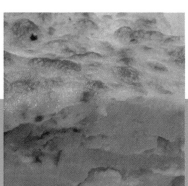 

❖ **SIDESHOW** ❖

CHEESY POTATOES

INGREDIENTS:

2 pounds frozen hashed browns
(thawed about 4 hours)

1 cup diced onions

1-pound carton of sour cream

8 oz. package sharp cheddar
cheese (shredded)

1 can cream of chicken soup

1 stick melted butter
(or margarine)

1 cup crushed potato chips

Salt and pepper to taste

I've seen variations of this recipe in a lot of places, but the first person I ever knew who made *Cheesy Potatoes* was Grandma Irene Delonis, a lovely little Polish lady. I'm not saying she invented the dish... she just made a good one. You can make this two ways: with frozen hashed browns or with real potatoes, which has a very different look. Try it both ways.

CHEESY POTATOES (MADE WITH HASHED BROWNS)

Directions:

Preheat oven to 375°. Mix all ingredients except potato chips. Pour into 9x13 baking dish. Sprinkle with crumbled chips and bake for 1 hour.

CHEESY POTATOES
(MADE WITH REAL POTATOES)

INGREDIENTS:

8 or 10 Yukon Gold potatoes

1 cup diced onions

1-pound carton of sour cream

1 can cream of chicken soup

1 stick melted butter or margarine

16-ounce bag cheddar cheese (shredded)

Garlic powder

Salt and pepper

I use Yukon Gold potatoes because the skin is light (so you don't have to peel them) and to me they are more flavorful than baking potatoes. This dish is great in a large casserole for a crowd or cut into elegant squares. You can play with the amounts depending upon how much you are making. But let's start small.

Directions:

Preheat oven to 400°. Wash potatoes and boil for about 25 minutes until soft and tender. Cut them into thin slices— not potato chip thin, but more thin than thick.

In a large bowl mix together onions, sour cream, cream of chicken soup, and butter. In a baking dish or casserole, spread a thin layer of the cream mixture. Add a layer of potato slices. Sprinkle with garlic powder, pepper, and cheddar cheese. Repeat these layers until the dish is filled to the top. Finish with a light layer of the creamy mixture. Cover with foil. Bake in a 350° oven for about one hour. Remove foil. Sprinkle on some shredded cheddar and return to oven for 5-10 minutes (or until cheese melts).

CORN ON THE COB

Whether you boil or grill corn on the cob, the most common mistake is overcooking. Boiling is probably the easier method. Fill a large pot with water. Add a ½ cup of sugar and bring to a boil. Add the corn (with husks removed). Boil for about five minutes. Done.

I prefer corn on the grill. Many people grill corn in the husk. I don't for two reasons. One, it's hard to husk hot corn. And two, you miss out on the slight charring on the kernels which is pleasing to the eye. I recommend you get rid of the husk and strings before cooking. Soak the cobs in water sweetened with sugar. Place the corncobs on a hot grill. Roast for about four minutes. Baste with melted butter and roll the cobs over 1/3. Cook another four minutes. Baste and roll 1/3. Cook the final four minutes and remove from the heat. Brush with melted butter and serve...or use a sharp knife to cut the kernels off the cobs.

FRIED POTATOES

Fried potatoes make a great breakfast side dish with scrambled eggs or an omelet. Add a toasted bagel. Maybe add some breakfast sausage. Yum!

Directions:
Boil some water in a large pan. Cook redskin potatoes for about 25 minutes or until tender. Slice the potatoes and set them aside. In a frying pan, melt butter over medium heat. Add green onions and diced pepper. Cook for about two minutes. Add potatoes. Mix well and cook for about five minutes stirring to avoid sticking to the pan. Salt and pepper to taste.

GRILLED GARLIC REDSKIN POTATOES

Grilling, garlic, and potatoes. You can't miss with that combination. The key here is that the potatoes are fully cooked when they go on the grill.

Directions:
Part one of the recipe is to boil the potatoes (with the skin on). Cook them for approximately 25 minutes or until tender. Drain potatoes and set aside. In a small bowl, melt butter and mix in garlic powder. Now you're ready for the grill. Set out potatoes on the hot grate. While they roast (getting those delightful little char marks) brush lightly with the mixture of melted butter and garlic powder. This will smoke some, but that just adds to the flavor. Roll the potatoes a couple of times to grill evenly, each time brushing lightly with the butter. Ten minutes total should do it.

Fried Potatoes

Grilled Garlic Redskin Potatoes

MASHED POTATOES
(GARLIC AND CHEDDAR)

INGREDIENTS:

large baking potatoes peeled and chopped into large pieces

OR

6-8 Yukon Gold potatoes with the skin on.

4 tablespoons butter (softened)

1 teaspoon garlic powder

¼ cup whole milk (room temperature)

1 cup shredded Cheddar cheese

2 tablespoons parsley

Salt

Freshly ground black pepper to taste

I haven't given much thought to an afterlife. But, assuming there is a heaven... and, assuming that I somehow get there— I know they will have garlic and cheddar mashed potatoes. I have never met a potato that I didn't like: baked, fried, scalloped, au gratin, hashed browns, French fries, potato salad... I could go on for hours. But right now, let's focus on my personal favorite.

Directions:

Fill a large pot about half way with water and bring to a boil. Place potato pieces in the water. When the water returns to a boil, cook for about 20 minutes or until the potato pieces are tender. Drain potatoes and return to the pan. Add butter, salt, and garlic powder. As you mash the potatoes, add milk. Sprinkle in cheddar cheese and parsley. Blend until melted and smooth. Salt and pepper to taste.

MASHED POTATO BAR

I have to admit that I didn't come up with this idea. Saw this setup at a wedding reception at a hotel someplace. I've done it for several holiday parties and it's always a big hit. The setup is simple. Put out a large pan or bowl of mashed potatoes. Surround it with small serving dishes with toppings. Then turn your guests loose to build their own concoction. *Tip: Buy some champagne glasses and use those for serving.

INGREDIENTS:

Yukon Gold, Redskins, or Sweet Potatoes (peeled).

teaspoon salt

butter

milk

Directions:

Place potato pieces in a large pot of boiling water. Add ½ teaspoon of salt. Boil 20-25 minutes or until tender (a fork can easily poke through). Drain water but keep potatoes in the pot. Add salt, butter and milk (amount depends upon how many potatoes you use). Mash until smooth.

Toppings Bar: (each gets its own serving bowl)

Brown gravy (Try adding sautéed mushrooms and a splash of red wine)
Chicken or turkey gravy
Butter (softened)
Sour cream
Shredded Cheddar cheese
Bacon (fried and crumbled)

SPINACH IS YOUR FRIEND
(POPEYE WAS RIGHT)

INGREDIENTS:

SAUTÉED SPINACH
Fresh washed spinach leaves
(a big pile will cook down
to a little, so use a lot)

2 tablespoons
Canola or Olive oil

¼ cup minced onion

1 teaspoon minced garlic

1 teaspoon butter

lemon juice

CREAMED SPINACH
4 cups cooked chopped
spinach (Fresh or Frozen)

2 tablespoons butter

2 tablespoons flour

1 cup whole milk,
or half and half

2 tablespoons finely
chopped onion

1 teaspoon minced garlic

½ cup sour cream

1 teaspoon *The Spice Blend*

¼ cup Parmesan cheese

I don't want to sound like your mother, but it is impossible to overstate the health benefits of fresh spinach. It aids in digestion, maintains low blood sugar, and curbs overeating. Spinach is a cancer fighter filled with vitamin C, vitamin E, and beta-carotene, powerful antioxidants that combat the onset of osteoporosis, high blood pressure, and cataracts. Okay, enough with the Mayo clinic sales pitch.

Directions:
In a large heated pan, add 2 tablespoons of olive oil. Add onion and minced garlic. Cook about 2 minutes. Add fresh spinach and saute until spinach is wilted and soft (about three minutes). Squeeze on a splash of lemon juice. Stir in butter and serve.

(Not as Healthy...but oh so delicious) Creamed Spinach:
First you make a Béchamel sauce.

Béchamel Sauce
2 tablespoons butter or margarine
2 tablespoons all-purpose flour
1 cup of whole milk (or half and half)

Directions:
In a small pan warm the milk. In a separate pan over medium heat melt butter. Add flour and blend until golden and smooth. Add warm milk a little at a time stirring constantly until mixture becomes smooth.

Putting It All Together:
In a different pan melt a tablespoon butter. Add onions and garlic. Cook for about 2 minutes until onions are soft. Add cooked (drained) spinach. Blend in Béchamel sauce, sour cream, salt, *The Spice Blend*, and Parmesan cheese. Heat for 3-5 minutes until mixture is hot.

STUFFING V. DRESSING

INGREDIENTS:

PLAIN OLE STUFFING
1 loaf of white bread torn into small pieces

¾ cup butter

1 cup onions (minced)

1 cup celery (minced)

2 tablespoons dried sage leaves

1 cup chicken broth

½ teaspoon ground black pepper

RAISIN AND APPLE STUFFING
1 loaf of white bread torn into small pieces

¾ cup butter

1 cup onions (minced)

1 cup celery (minced)

2 tablespoons dried sage leaves

1 cup chicken broth

½ teaspoon ground black pepper

½ cup apples (diced)

¾ cup dark raisins

SAUSAGE STUFFING
1 loaf of white bread torn into small piece)

1 lb. bulk sage sausage (you'll find it with the breakfast sausage at the grocery)

¾ cup butter

1 cup onions (minced)

1 cup celery (minced)

2 tablespoons dried sage leaves

1 cup chicken broth

½ teaspoon ground black pepper

This is not a landmark Supreme Court case, but a long time debate. Stuffing is arguably the standout dish at Thanksgiving, but is shrouded in ambiguity. I've read that if it's cooked inside the bird it's stuffing, and if cooked in a casserole, it's dressing. Down south, it's called dressing no matter how you prepare it.

Among the more important considerations are health issues. Many experts now recommend that you don't stuff a bird because stuffing will soak up the raw juice which may carry E. coli. And it's more difficult to know when a stuffed bird is sufficiently cooked. I've made stuffing in a casserole for years, and haven't gotten any complaints.

Plain Ole Stuffing
Directions:

Melt butter in a saucepan over medium heat. Add onions and celery. Sauté for about five minutes until soft. In a large bowl, combine that mixture with crumbled bread and all other ingredients. Blend well. Bake in a covered casserole at 350° for 30 minutes. You can add a little broth at the end if you want your stuffing more moist.

Raisin and Apple Stuffing:
Tip: Soak raisins in a pan of warm water until you need them. Dice the apples just before you use them to avoid having them turn brown.

Directions:

Melt butter in a saucepan over medium heat. Add onions and celery. Sauté for about five minutes until soft. In a large bowl, combine that mixture with crumbled bread and all other ingredients. Mix well. Bake in a covered casserole at 350° for 30 minutes.

Sausage Stuffing
Directions:

Brown the sausage and break it up into very small pieces, or better yet, give it a quick spin in the food processor. Melt butter in a saucepan over medium heat. Add onions and celery. Sauté for about five minutes or until soft. In a large bowl, combine that mixture with crumbled bread, the sausage, and all other ingredients. Blend well. Bake in a covered casserole at 350° for 30 minutes.

STUFFED MUSHROOMS

INGREDIENTS:

BACON STUFFED MUSHROOMS

8-10 large fresh mushrooms

6 bacon slices

1 tablespoon butter or margarine

¼ cup minced onion

¼ cup minced celery

¾ cup of breadcrumbs

1 teaspoon sage

½ teaspoon salt

¼ teaspoon pepper

½ cup shredded cheddar cheese.

¼ cup white wine

CRABMEAT STUFFED MUSHROOMS

3 tablespoons butter or margarine

8-10 large fresh mushrooms

2 tablespoons minced green onions

1 teaspoon lemon juice

1 small can crabmeat

½ cup breadcrumbs

1 egg, beaten

½ teaspoon dried dill

¾ cup shredded Monterey Jack cheese

¼ cup white wine

Stuffed mushrooms are another great side dish or an appetizer. If setting them out as a snack, use smaller mushroom caps, larger when served as a side dish. You have lots of options for the filling. Here are three of them.

Bacon Stuffed Mushrooms

Directions:
Wash mushrooms and remove stems. Set aside.

Fry bacon in a heavy skillet. When fairly crisp, remove and set on paper towel to drain. Crumble bacon. In the same pan where you cooked the bacon, add a tablespoon of butter and sauté onions and celery.

In a large bowl, combine breadcrumbs, bacon, sautéed onions and celery, sage, salt, pepper, cheddar cheese and white wine. Mix thoroughly. Press mixture into mushroom caps, mounding slightly. Bake, uncovered about 20 minutes and 350°.

Crabmeat Stuffed Mushrooms

Directions:
Preheat oven to 350°.

Melt butter in a medium saucepan over medium heat. Stir in green onions and cook until soft (about 3 minutes). Remove saucepan from heat. Stir in lemon juice, crabmeat, breadcrumbs, egg, dill, and cheese. Thoroughly blend the mixture.

Stuff mushroom caps and place in a baking dish. Bake uncovered about 20 minutes, until lightly browned. Serve warm.

INGREDIENTS:

SAUSAGE STUFFED MUSHROOMS

8-10 large fresh mushrooms

3 tablespoons olive oil

¾ pound ground Italian sausage

¼ cup minced green onions

1 teaspoon minced garlic

¼ cup Marsala wine or (your favorite white wine)

½ cup breadcrumbs

½ cup freshly grated Parmesan

¼ cup shredded mozzarella cheese

2 tablespoons minced fresh parsley leaves

Salt and freshly ground black pepper

Sausage Stuffed Mushrooms

Directions:

Preheat oven to 350°. Wash mushrooms and remove stems. Set aside. Heat oil in a medium size pan over medium heat. Add sausage and cook 8 to 10 minutes, stirring frequently, until it's completely browned. Stir in minced green onions and garlic. Cook for another 2 to 3 minutes. Add wine, breadcrumbs, Parmesan and mozzarella cheese, and parsley. Continue cooking until cheese has melted and made the sausage mixture a little gooey. Fill each mushroom generously with the sausage mixture. Arrange the mushrooms in a baking dish. Bake 20 minutes until lightly browned.

VEGGIES ON THE GRILL

The worst way to prepare vegetables is to boil them. They lose nutrients, color, flavor, firmness, and texture. The only vegetables I can think of that survive boiling well are carrots, potatoes, peas, and spinach. Steaming is good...but grilling is better.

The best vegetables for grilling are: zucchini, asparagus, mushrooms, and bell peppers—onions get tricky when the slices start to fall apart. Because vegetables have no fat, you need to marinate or season, and brush with a little oil before they go on the grill. Cut peppers into thirds. Cut zucchini into lengthwise slices. Leave mushrooms whole, but remove the stems. Asparagus just needs a little oil and pepper. And make sure you break off the tough stems.

Like grilling meat, avoid the temptation to push, poke, and move your veggies around the grill. Close the lid and let them cook for 3-5 minutes. Turn them over for another 3-5 minutes. Done.

➤ DESSERTS ◄

ANICA'S CHOCOLATE CHIP COOKIES

INGREDIENTS:

1½ cups butter

1 cup light brown sugar

1 cup sugar

2 eggs

1 teaspoon vanilla

1 tablespoon water

3 cups flour

1 teaspoon salt

1 teaspoon baking soda

2 cups chocolate morsels

Do you know who invented the chocolate chip cookie? No it wasn't my wife's friend Anica. It was Ruth Graves Wakefield of Whitman, Massachusetts, back in 1937. It happened by accident when she ran out of baker's chocolate and substituted a semi-sweet chocolate bar cut up into bits. Much to her surprise, the pieces didn't melt and blend in, but only got soft. She served them anyway... and the rest, as they say, is history.

There are hundreds of chocolate chip cookie recipes out there, and this one is probably not significantly different. So, if you already have a favorite, go for it. The key to a great chocolate chip cookie is in the baking more than the ingredients.

Directions:

Preheat oven to 375°. Cream butter with brown sugar and white granulated sugar. Add eggs, vanilla, and water. Mix thoroughly. In a separate bowl, combine flour, salt, and baking soda. Add these dry ingredients to the other bowl and mix well. Stir in chocolate morsels. Spoon onto a baking sheet.

**Here comes the important part. *Don't over bake your cookies.* Allow me to say that one more time. *Don't over bake your cookies.* They will continue to bake for a minute or two after you remove them from the oven. Consider this in your timing. Teaspoon size drop cookies should bake about 8 minutes for chewy, 10 minutes for firm. If you're making larger cookies, adjust your time accordingly. You'll have to experiment a little. Always err on the side of chewy when it comes to chocolate chip cookies. Once they get crispy, you might as well buy a bag at the grocery store. After you remove cookies from the oven, allow sufficient time for them to cool so they don't tear apart trying to get them off the pan. *Tip: Use parchment (or baking) paper on your cookie sheet. Cookies will bake more evenly, your cookie sheet stays clean, and you don't have to scrape cookies off the pan.

BAILEY'S SHAKE

INGREDIENTS:

Chocolate ice cream

Whole milk

Baileys Irish Cream

Whipped cream

Hershey's Chocolate bar
or chocolate syrup

Large Martini glass
(in freezer for at least
one hour before serving)

A Bailey's shake is great any time of year, though I tend to save it for gatherings around Christmas-- maybe because that's the time of year for extravagance. Obviously this is a dessert for adults. For children in the crowd simply omit the Bailey's. Don't fret over measuring exact amounts. With these ingredients, you can't go wrong.

Directions:

Put several scoops of chocolate ice cream, a generous splash of milk and equally generous splash of Baileys in a blender. Whip it up until smooth. Pour into a large frozen glass. Top with whipped cream. Finish it off with a drizzle of chocolate syrup, or shavings from a chocolate bar. Maybe some festive sprinkles. Get creative!

BANANA BREAD (GRANDPA KLOKA'S)

INGREDIENTS:

1 cup margarine (soft)

2½ cups sugar

6 well-beaten eggs

2 teaspoons baking soda

1 cup sour cream

2½ cups mashed bananas
(use 4 or 5 ripe bananas)

3 cups unsifted
all-purpose flour

2 (9x5) bread pans

This recipe (passed down from my wife's grandfather) might be 100 years old, and it's still the best banana bread I've ever had. At Christmas, I make several batches in small bread pans, and send them with a Christmas card for my family. It's a simple recipe. The only mistake you might make is not blending in the flour well enough. I did that once and was mortified when friends and family found tiny flour balls in each slice.

Directions:

Pre-heat oven to 325°. Prepare your pans: With your fingers, coat the sides and bottom of bread pans with a light coating of margarine. Put a heaping tablespoon of flour into the pan and shake it around to put a film of flour on all sides and bottom. Dump out excess.

Prepare batter: In a large mixing bowl, cream butter and sugar until light and fluffy. Add eggs and beat at medium speed for two minutes. In a separate bowl, combine sour cream and baking soda. Add that mixture to the butter and eggs mixture. Add bananas and beat until combined.

Now add flour one cup at a time beating well after each cup. After flour is completely blended, beat well for another 2 minutes. You don't want any stray flour balls floating around in there. Pour mixture into pans and bake at 325° for about 50 minutes. Test for doneness: Push down in the center gently. Cake should bounce back and a toothpick should come out clean.

CAKE POPS!

INGREDIENTS:

1 box of cake mix

1 can of cake frosting

2 packages of candy melts
or candy coating

Assorted sprinkles

Cake pop sticks

A thick sheet of Styrofoam

Any high class cookbook will include a recipe for truffles. Thank goodness we don't have to worry about this being a high class cookbook. But you should at least know what a truffle is. You have two choices.

1. A strong-smelling underground fungus.

2. A soft candy or cake-like dessert often covered with chocolate.

Let's work with #2. A chocolate truffle bears the name because of the physical resemblance to the strong-smelling underground fungus... not because the dessert actually includes fungus. So, if you ask me, it's a dumb name for an otherwise awesome desert. Let's do a variation on the theme—Cake Pops!

For the coating you'll need candy melts or other chocolate made specifically for coating fruit, pretzels, cookies, or cake pops. Don't use chocolate chips or Hershey bars. You can find candy coating chocolate in the baking aisle of the grocery store, or the baking/candy section of most craft stores.

Directions:

Bake cake according to directions on the box— chocolate cake, white cake, yellow cake. It doesn't matter. Allow cake to cool. Crumble it into a large bowl. Blend in a can of frosting. My favorite is red velvet cake and chocolate frosting.

Set that bowl aside and start melting your candy coat chocolate. The package will say you can microwave it, but I've never had good luck with that. I use a double boiler. Warm chocolate until melted. Add a little cooking oil to thin if necessary.

Roll the cake mixture into meatball size balls and spread them out on a cookie sheet. Take a cake pop stick and dip it about an inch into the chocolate and then into a cake ball. When all sticks are planted, put the cookie sheet in the freezer for fifteen minutes. This helps the ball stay on the stick when you dip it into the chocolate in the next step.

Dip each ball into the chocolate and allow excess to drip off. Add sprinkles while the chocolate is wet. Plant your cake pop in the Styrofoam block to dry. You can use additional frosting and a cake decorator to add more details if you like. Go online. You'll find lots of great ideas. It takes a little practice and patience to develop an efficient technique, but it's worth it. This a great family activity, and wow are they popular.

DIRT DESSERT

INGREDIENTS:

1 package Oreo cookies

1 package instant chocolate pudding

1 (8-ounce) package cream cheese (softened)

1 container whipped dessert topping

1 package gummy worms (optional)

1 medium sized flowerpot

1 artificial flower

Not much cooking involved in this recipe. This is mostly about presentation. It's a huge hit with kids. We did this for a couple of birthday parties when our daughters were little. Put the flowerpots on the table before the kids sit down. When it comes time for dessert, they expect presentation of a cake. Aren't they surprised when you tell them the flower centerpieces are the dessert. And they *really* love the worms.

Directions:

Crush Oreos to a fine texture to resemble potting soil. Set aside. Mix the package of chocolate pudding as indicated on box. In a separate bowl, blend together softened cream cheese and whipped topping. Now it's like building lasagna in the flowerpot. Start with a layer of crushed Oreos. Next layer is the cream cheese mixture. Next layer is pudding. Repeat: Oreos, cream cheese, and pudding. Now sprinkle remaining crumbled cookies on top. It's best to make this the day before so you can refrigerate over night. Add an artificial flower and some gummy worms poking from the surface.

MARTIN AND BESSIE'S CHRISTMAS COOKIES

INGREDIENTS:

1 cup butter softened (no margarine substitution allowed in this recipe)

1 cup sugar

1 egg

1 tablespoon vanilla extract

3 cups flour

½ teaspoon baking powder

½ teaspoon salt

Wax paper

Parchment paper

Cookie sheets

Sprinkles and cookie cutters

Turn this project into a family gathering. Everyone should bring their favorite cookie cutters and a shirt box or two to take home their share of finished cookies. Put on some Christmas music and have at it! Martin and Bessie were my wife's grandparents. They made these cookies by the hundreds and left a legacy of warm memories.

The recipe is not complicated. The trick is freezing the dough slightly so that the cookies can maintain a shape when you cut them (since they're almost pure butter). You can double, or triple the recipe to make lots of cookies.

Directions:

In a large bowl cream together butter and sugar until light and fluffy. Beat in eggs and vanilla. In a separate bowl, combine flour and salt. Stir dry ingredients into wet ingredients and blend. Preheat oven to 350°.

Place a sheet of wax paper on a cookie sheet or piece of strong cardboard. Using a floured rolling pin, roll out dough into a sheet about 1/8 inch thick. Put the sheet of cookie dough in the freezer for about ten minutes. This will make the dough firm enough to cut. Use cookie cutters to make a variety of shapes.

Cover a cookie sheet with parchment paper. Place cookies one-inch apart on the sheet and bake for 8 to 10 minutes, until lightly browned. While they're baking, re-roll the trimmings, place in the freezer and repeat the cutting and baking process. Transfer cookies to wire rack to decorate with sprinkles and cool.

MEAGHAN'S AWESOMELY CHEWY OATMEAL COOKIES

INGREDIENTS:

1 cup flour

1 teaspoon baking powder

½ teaspoon baking soda

½ teaspoon salt

½ teaspoon ground cinnamon

2 tablespoon margarine at room temperature

½ cup sugar

½ cup brown sugar

1 egg

¼ cup mashed ripe banana

½ teaspoon vanilla extract

2 cups quick oats

¾ cup raisins

Meaghan is a producer at the TV station where I work. She's also a mom who shared this low fat recipe that is both healthful and gooey delicious. As with most cookies, the key is to err on the side of "under-baking". You want these to be chewy not dry.

Directions:

Preheat oven to 350°. Cover a baking pan with a sheet of parchment paper. In a medium bowl, mix together flour, baking powder, baking soda, salt and cinnamon. In a separate bowl, cream together butter and the sugars. Use an electric mixer if you have one. Add the egg, mashed banana, and vanilla extract. Stir in the flour mixture and the oats until well blended. Now add the raisins. Drop heaping tablespoons of dough onto the baking sheet. Bake for about 8-10 minutes depending on thickness. Remove from oven. If you're not sure the cookies are done, always err on the side of gooey rather than dry.

(MAGGIE'S) ZUCCHINI BREAD

INGREDIENTS:

4 eggs beaten

2½ cups sugar

2 tablespoons vanilla

3 cups shredded zucchini

1¼ cups vegetable oil

1 tablespoon cinnamon

1½ teaspoons salt

1½ teaspoons baking soda

½ teaspoon baking powder

3 cups flour

2 (9x5) bread pans

Zucchini bread is a close cousin to banana bread, though I tend to separate them by seasons: banana bread in the winter and zucchini bread in the summer. If you have a garden, you know that zucchini is easy to grow. And while I love grilled zucchini, you need something else to do with them. This is a delicious alternative. I got this recipe from a wonderful neighbor back in Jackson, Michigan about 30 years ago. Maggie, if you stumble upon this book… thanks.

Directions:
Preheat over to 325°.

Prepare Zucchini: Shred zucchini the old fashion way, with a hand grater. If you use a food processor the pulp gets too soupy. And, use the skin as well (adds nice specks of color to the bread). The number of zucchini you need to get three cups of pulp depends on their size.

Prepare your pans: With your fingers, coat the sides and bottom of the bread pans with a light coating of butter. Put a tablespoon of flour into the pan and shake it around to put a film of flour on all sides and bottom. Dump out excess.

Prepare the batter: In a large bowl, beat eggs sugar and vanilla. Blend in zucchini and oil. Sprinkle in cinnamon, salt, baking soda, and baking powder. Now add flour ***one cup at a time*** blending well after each cup. Pour mixture into pans and bake at 325° for about one hour.

Test for doneness: Push down in center gently. Cake should bounce back and a toothpick should come out clean.